PRECISIONISM IN AMERICA
1915–1941: REORDERING REALITY

PRECISIONISM IN AMERICA
1915–1941: REORDERING REALITY

Harry N. Abrams, Inc., Publishers in association with The Montclair Art Museum

Frontispiece:
Charles Sheeler. *Upper Deck.* 1929. Oil on canvas, 29¼ x 22½".
Fogg Art Museum, Harvard University Art Museums, Cambridge,
Massachusetts, Louise E. Bettens Fund (fig. 10)

Published on the occasion of the exhibition *Precisionism in America 1915–1941: Reordering Reality,* organized by The Montclair Art Museum, New Jersey.

The exhibition and accompanying publication have been made possible by The Henry Luce Foundation, Inc., The National Endowment for the Arts, a federal agency, and the Merrill Lynch and Co. Foundation, Inc. Museum programs are made possible in part by generous funding from the New Jersey State Council on the Arts, Department of State.

Itinerary

The Montclair Art Museum, New Jersey
November 20, 1994–January 22, 1995

Norton Gallery of Art, West Palm Beach, Florida
February 11–April 2, 1995

Columbus Museum of Art, Ohio
May 7–July 4, 1995

Sheldon Memorial Art Gallery, Lincoln, Nebraska
September 5–November 5, 1995

Project Manager: Margaret L. Kaplan
Editor: Diana Murphy
Designer: Darilyn Lowe Carnes

Library of Congress Cataloging-in-Publication Data
Precisionism in America. 1915–1941: reordering reality.
p. cm.
Exhibition catalog.
Includes bibliographical references and index.
ISBN 0-8109-3734-4
1. Precisionism—United States—Exhibitions. 2. Art, American—Exhibitions. 3. Art, Modern—20th century—United States—Exhibitions.
N6512.5.P67P7 1994
709'.73'09041—dc20 94-4368
CIP

Published in 1994 by Harry N. Abrams, Incorporated, New York
A Times Mirror Company

Printed and bound in Japan

TABLE OF CONTENTS

Charles Sheeler. *Home Sweet Home.* 1931. Oil on canvas, 36 x 29¼".
The Detroit Institute of Arts. Gift of Robert H. Tannahill (fig. 13)

FOREWORD

ONE OF THE GREAT paintings in the collection of The Montclair Art Museum is *Queensborough Bridge*, a Precisionist work by Elsie Driggs. It was to that painting that my thoughts immediately turned when Gail Stavitsky walked into my office at The Museum of Modern Art, New York, weeks before I assumed the directorship in Montclair, and described the Precisionist exhibition she wished to organize. What better way to draw attention to our collection, contribute to scholarship on American art, and underscore our leadership role in the world of museums? I immediately agreed (subject to ever-elusive funding, of course).

That was two years ago, and Ms. Stavitsky and the rest of our staff have worked unflaggingly on the exhibition and catalogue since then. It gives me enormous personal pleasure and pride to see our early dreams so thoroughly realized.

I have had complete confidence in Ms. Stavitsky's abilities, having known her since we were students together at New York University's Institute of Fine Arts. She is a fine scholar and teacher, as well as a tireless administrator. We all knew what an organizational challenge *Precisionism in America 1915–1941: Reordering Reality* would present, especially for such a small staff. But we counted on her professionalism and stamina to see us through, and we were never disappointed. Gail agreed to serve as Acting Curator of MAM when that position was vacated, and her wisdom and judgment aided us immeasurably. We are enormously indebted to her.

It is no secret that special project funding is harder than ever to come by during these trying economic times. It was the willingness of the Henry Luce Foundation, Inc., to make an early commitment to *Precisionism in America* that enabled us to move ahead with our preparations. Special thanks are due to the Directors of the Foundation, to Mr. Luce himself, who has been such a champion of American art, and to Ellen Holtzman, the Foundation's Program Director for the Arts, whose encouragement and support have been so important to this project.

I am especially grateful to Margaret Kaplan, Executive Editor, and Paul Gottlieb, Publisher, of Harry N. Abrams, Inc., for believing in this project and investing in a much more ample catalogue than the museum could have managed on its own. I have worked with both of them over the past eighteen years in a variety of roles and my respect and affection for them has grown in the preparation of *Precisionism in America*. I hope this will be the first of many joint ventures.

I would also like to thank Merribell Parsons, former Director of the Columbus Museum of Art, Ohio; Christina Orr-Cahall, Director of the Norton Gallery of Art, West Palm Beach, Florida; and George Neubert, Director of the University of Nebraska Art Galleries–Sheldon Memorial Art Gallery, Lincoln, all of whom have agreed to host the exhibition during its 1995 tour.

Finally, I would like to thank the museum's Board of Trustees, whose belief in their new Director and her substantially new staff sustained all of us throughout the organization of this important exhibition. I think it fair to say that we have all learned a great deal about one another in the process and will have even greater confidence in our possibilities as we chart our future plans.

Ellen S. Harris
Director
The Montclair Art Museum
February 10, 1994

INTRODUCTION AND ACKNOWLEDGMENTS

IN 1927 AND 1929, Alfred H. Barr Jr., future director of The Museum of Modern Art, New York, featured the work of the "Precisionists" Charles Sheeler and Charles Demuth in his lectures on major tendencies in modern American painting. He and other critics coined this term to characterize stylistic, thematic consistencies among certain progressive artists, who never actually formed a declared group or school. Loosely linked through friendships and associations with particular New York galleries, these painters and photographers shared sources of inspiration and aesthetic vocabularies.

By establishing links between America's past and present, the Precisionists affirmed the country's pervasive quest for national identity. Not only were they among the first to adapt their selectively realist styles to the precise geometry of the burgeoning machine age, but they also spearheaded the revival of interest in America's fine art, folk art, and applied art traditions. Far from being a provincial phenomenon, Precisionism must also be seen within the international avant-garde context of the classicizing "call to order" after the destructive chaos of World War I. Thus the movement developed vital bridges between native traditions of realism and such European influences as Cézanne, Cubism, Purism, and the Renaissance masters.

At the core of the Precisionists' classic, objectivist aesthetic was an exacting synthesis of realism and abstract design. They reordered local reality to reveal its universal architectonic structures beneath the fluctuations of experience. Static, sharply defined, simplified, smoothly brushed forms in unmodulated colors were disengaged from transitory aspects of painterly process, time, atmosphere, and sentiment. Suppressing anecdotal detail and the human presence to embrace the direct, impersonal apprehension of objects, the Precisionists were perhaps the most sensitive barometers of their era. Sometimes they manifested ambivalent attitudes toward mechanization, standardization, and dehumanization; nevertheless, they adapted the clean lines and unadorned functional clarity of the urban-industrial environment. The Precisionists found the same attributes of beauty in early American rural architecture and folk art, and they established a vernacular heritage for the country's machine age. Through their various contributions, the Precisionists forged one of America's most significant art movements between the wars. Their considerable achievements debunk lingering interpretations of this period as a time of nativist backlash and retreat from modernism awaiting the so-called triumph of American art in the 1940s.

For the first time, Precisionism is examined in this publication from a variety of vantage points, with essays on the impact of photography, the European perspective, literary parallels, and America's machine culture. I would like to thank Ellen Handy, Assistant Professor, Division of the Arts, Bard College; Miles Orvell, Professor of English and American Studies, Temple University; Romy Golan, Assistant Professor of Art History, Yale University; and Lisa Steinman, Professor of English and Humanities, Reed College, for their important statements, which provide a unique multidisciplinary examination of Precisionism's complexities. Ellen Handy was also particularly helpful in the selection of photographs for the show and Miles Orvell offered cogent editorial suggestions for my essay.

The origins of the exhibition—the first on the subject in twelve years—date back several years to discussions with Françoise Rambach. I am deeply grateful to her for suggesting the idea for this show and contributing to its realization. She and her husband, Harvey Rambach, are among the many generous lenders to the exhibition.

I would also especially like to thank Rick Stewart, Curator of Western Painting and Sculpture, Amon Carter Museum. His perceptive scholarship and redefinition of Precisionism have served as the inspirational foundation for my research and the title of the exhibition.

The concept for the show was presented to Ellen Harris, Director of The Montclair Art Museum, who has been tremendously creative, persistent, and supportive in its implementation. I would like to thank her very much as well as the museum staff, particularly Alejandro Anreus, former Curator of Collections and Exhibitions; Martin Beck, former Registrar; Randolph Black, Registrar; Leanne McGowan, Assistant to the Director; Anne-Marie Nolin, Director of Communications; Catherine Fazekas, Coordinator of Public Relations; and Development Director Elyse Reissman. This exhibition would not have been possible without their inexhaustible combined and individual efforts.

My thanks are also extended to the following museum staff members at the venues to which the exhibition will travel: Nannette V. Maciejunes, Curator of American Art, Columbus Museum of Art; Daphne Anderson Deeds, Curator and Assistant Director, Sheldon Memorial Art Gallery; David F. Setford, Senior Curator, and Olga M. Viso, Assistant Curator, Norton Gallery of Art. They have contributed enormously to the realization of this project. Nannette Maciejunes also provided excellent editorial suggestions for my essay.

I would like to express my gratitude to Diana Murphy, Senior Editor; Darilyn Lowe Carnes, Designer; and Shun Yamamoto, Vice President of Production, at Harry N. Abrams, Inc., for their judiciousness and skill in producing this beautiful publication. It is the only in-depth, interdisciplinary study in print on Precisionism.

Many other individuals and organizations deserve mention as well, especially the numerous museum and gallery staff members who facilitated our efforts to secure loans, acquire photographs, and conduct research. With apologies for not being able to name everyone in this regard, I would like to thank the following individuals: Innis H. Shoemaker, Senior Curator of Prints, Drawings, and Photographs, Martha Chahroudi, Associate Curator of Photographs, and Ann Temkin, Muriel and Philip Berman Curator of Twentieth-Century Art, Philadelphia Museum of Art; Maria Morris Hambourg, Curator in Charge, Department of Photographs, Colta F. Ives, Curator in Charge, Department of Prints and Illustrated Books, and William S. Lieberman, Jacques and Natasha Gelman Chairman, Department of Twentieth-Century Art, The Metropolitan Museum of Art, New York; Kirk Varnedoe, Director, Department of Paintings and Sculpture, and Peter Galassi, Director, Department of Photography, The Museum of Modern Art, New York; Adam D. Weinberg, Curator, Permanent Collection, Whitney Museum of American Art, New York; and Joseph Jacobs, Curator of Painting and Sculpture, The Newark Museum. The staff of the Archives of American Art, Smithsonian Institution, in New York and Washington, D.C., was very helpful, as was the Whitney Museum of American Art Library staff, especially Julie Mellby. My gratitude is also extended to the staff of the Museum of Modern Art Library, especially Rona Roob, Archivist. Special thanks are in order to Dr. Milton W. Brown, as well as two artists in the show, Edmund Lewandowski and Virginia Berresford, who all graciously shared their ideas with me in interviews.

Isabelle Dervaux, Marge Kline of the Philadelphia Museum of Art's Twentieth-Century Art Department, and Naomi Sawelson-Gorse have, as usual, been extremely helpful in a number of ways. I would like to thank Edward R. Downe Jr., Howard Greenberg, Janet Marqusee, Michael Rosenfeld, Suzanne Vanderwoude, Didi Wigmore, and Amy Wolf for their great assistance in securing loans for the show. Finally, I would like to acknowledge the following individuals for their generous and varied assistance: Betsy Aaron, William C. Agee, Ida Balboul, John Crawford, Earl Davis, Virginia Dodier, Marianne Doezema, Betsy Fahlman, Thomas C. Folk, Amanda Harvey, Arthur E. Imperatore, Wendy Jeffers, Norman Keyes, Adele Lozowick, Karen Lucic, Barbara Buhler Lynes, Virginia H. Marquardt, Lisa Messinger, Diana Dimodica Mille, Joann Moser, Francis Naumann, Erika Passantino, Glenn C. Peck, Daniel Robbins, Cora Rosevear, Henry Sayre, Richard Sheinaus, Suzanne Suba, Carol Troyen, Beth Venn, Susan Weininger, Elizabeth Wylie, Deborah Wythe, and Judith Zilczer.

Gail Stavitsky

Georgia O'Keeffe. *East River from the 30th Story of the Shelton Hotel*. 1928. Oil on canvas, 30 x 48". New Britain Museum of American Art, Connecticut. Stephen Lawrence Fund 1958.9 (plate 23)

LENDERS TO THE EXHIBITION

Albright-Knox Art Gallery, Buffalo, New York
Amon Carter Museum, Fort Worth, Texas
Anonymous Lenders
The Art Institute of Chicago, Illinois
The Art Museum, Princeton University, New Jersey
The Brooklyn Museum, New York
Canadian Centre for Architecture, Montreal
Columbus Museum of Art, Ohio
Dallas Museum of Art, Texas
Davison Art Center Collection, Wesleyan University, Middletown, Connecticut
The Detroit Institute of Arts, Michigan
The DeWoody Collection
George Eastman House, Rochester, New York
Ebsworth Collection, St. Louis, Missouri
Georgia Museum of Art, The University of Georgia, Athens
Gilman Paper Company, New York, New York
Lawrence J. Goldrich
Foster and Monique Goldstrom, New York, New York
Courtesy of James Graham & Sons, Inc., New York, New York
Courtesy Howard Greenberg Gallery, New York, New York
Samuel P. Harn Museum of Art, University of Florida, Gainesville
Hirshhorn Museum and Sculpture Garden, Smithsonian Institution, Washington, D.C.
Arthur E. Imperatore; courtesy Luhring Augustine Gallery, New York, New York
Edward J. Lenkin and Katherine L. Meier
Adele Lozowick
Ezra Mack, New York, New York
The Metropolitan Museum of Art, New York, New York
The Montclair Art Museum, New Jersey
Museum of Art, Rhode Island School of Design, Providence
Museum of Fine Arts, Boston, Massachusetts
The Museum of Modern Art, New York, New York
National Museum of American Art, Smithsonian Institution, Washington, D.C.
The Newark Museum, New Jersey
New Britain Museum of American Art, Connecticut
New Jersey State Museum, Trenton
New Orleans Museum of Art, Louisiana
Norton Gallery of Art, West Palm Beach, Florida
The Old Print Shop Inc., New York, New York
Philadelphia Museum of Art, Pennsylvania
The Phillips Collection, Washington, D.C.
Mr. and Mrs. Meyer P. Potamkin
Collection Françoise and Harvey Rambach
The Regis Collection, Minneapolis, Minnesota
Rose Art Museum, Brandeis University, Waltham, Massachusetts
Michael Rosenfeld Gallery, New York, New York
Courtesy Salander O'Reilly Galleries, New York, New York
Sheldon Memorial Art Gallery, University of Nebraska–Lincoln
The David and Alfred Smart Museum of Art, The University of Chicago, Illinois
Collection William F. Stewart, Atlanta, Georgia
Marjorie S. and Leonard Vernon
The Whitney Museum of American Art, New York, New York
Williams College Museum of Art, Williamstown, Massachusetts
Worcester Art Museum, Massachusetts
Yale University Art Gallery, New Haven, Connecticut

REORDERING REALITY:
Precisionist Directions in American Art, 1915–1941

Gail Stavitsky

ORIGINS OF PRECISIONISM

IN 1915, AMERICA'S DESTINY as the next artistic center was proclaimed by Marcel Duchamp. Having emigrated from war-torn France, he embraced America's "cold and scientific" life, observing that "the art of Europe is finished—dead—and that America is the country of the art of the future. . . . Look at the skyscrapers! Has Europe anything to show more beautiful than these?"[1] His colleague Francis Picabia concurred: "Since machinery is the soul of the modern world," he argued, "and since the genius of machinery attains its highest expression in America, why is it not reasonable to believe that in America the art of the future will flower most brilliantly?"[2]

Hailed as the "world's new art center," New York became the site of fertile exchanges between French and American modernists. One of the key meeting places was the home of the avant-garde collectors Walter and Louise Arensberg. Among their regular circle of writers and artists were Duchamp, Picabia, Albert Gleizes, William Carlos Williams, and the following young American painters who were later regarded as Precisionists: Charles Sheeler, Charles Demuth, Joseph Stella, and Morton Schamberg. Since his arrival in June 1915, Duchamp had been the star attraction of this lively, iconoclastic salon, which became identified with the New York Dada movement.

Appreciating Duchamp's impersonal, intellectual approach to artmaking, Sheeler described him as being "built with the precision . . . of an instrument for making scientific measurements. . . . [having] declared himself through with painting."[3] Sheeler also spoke of Duchamp's *The Bride Stripped Bare by Her Bachelors, Even (The Large Glass)* (fig. 1), which he and Demuth admired for its concept and meticulous craftsmanship: "Whatever he touched . . . had a most beautiful precision."[4] Duchamp himself referred to his complex, philosophical fusion of the sexual and the mechanical as "painting of precision, and beauty of indifference."[5] This objectivist effort to embody the unadorned reality of things is related to such studies for *The Large Glass* as the two *Chocolate Grinder* paintings, exhibited in 1915 at the Carroll Galleries in New York and hanging on the walls of the Arensberg apartment by 1918. The original study for the "Bachelor Apparatus," *Chocolate Grinder, No. 1* (fig. 2) could be regarded as the first Precisionist painting, in terms

1. Marcel Duchamp. *The Bride Stripped Bare by Her Bachelors, Even (The Large Glass)*, front view. 1915–23. Oil and lead wire on glass, 109¼ x 69⅛". Philadelphia Museum of Art. Bequest of Katherine S. Dreier

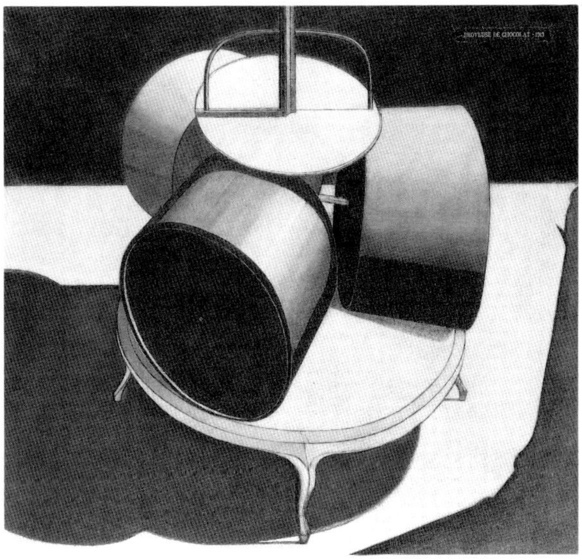

2. Marcel Duchamp. *Chocolate Grinder, No. 1.* 1913. Oil on canvas, 24 x 25". Philadelphia Museum of Art. Louise and Walter Arensberg Collection

of its clearly defined, static, simplified forms, isolated on a blank ground and described by Duchamp as being like a mechanical drawing—"an architectural, dry rendering . . . purified of all past influences."[6]

The first American to develop the potential of America's mechanistic environment into a Precisionist aesthetic was Morton Schamberg. As early as 1912, Schamberg had discussed with his lifelong friend Sheeler pictures of mechanical subjects that he wanted to paint. His own experiences as a photographer and as an architecture student at the University of Pennsylvania from 1899 to 1903 were influential, as was his trip abroad with Sheeler in 1908–9. There the young artists appreciated the timeless architectural structure in the paintings of such Renaissance masters as Giotto, Masaccio, and Piero della Francesca. They found these same principles, emphasizing essentials and the necessity of an underlying structure, in the art of Cézanne, Picasso, and Matisse, seen in Paris and, back in New York, at the landmark Armory Show of 1913. Inspired to abandon the spontaneous bravura technique of their former teacher, William Merritt Chase, both Schamberg and Sheeler emerged as important American Cubists between 1913 and 1915.

By early 1915, Schamberg had created a loosely brushed rendition of a telephone, which, as William C. Agee has observed, predated Francis Picabia's famous machine paintings by several months. Nevertheless, the clarification of Schamberg's images of isolated, precisely rendered machinery in 1916 has been linked by Agee to Duchamp's *Chocolate Grinder, No. 1* and Picabia's schematic machine portraits. Schamberg probably saw Picabia's renowned image of pioneering photographer and dealer Alfred Stieglitz depicted as a folding camera published in *291* (plate 1). This avant-garde periodical was named after Stieglitz's legendary gallery, which had introduced Picasso and other modern artists to America before the war.

Featuring other mechanomorphic works by Picabia as well, *291* promoted the "age of the machine," the "element of reason," and the "scientific influence in art."[7] One of the chief contributors to *291* was the caricaturist Marius de Zayas, who praised the straight photography of Stieglitz as a paradigm for the "desire of modern plastic expression . . . to create for itself an objectivity."[8] In New York de Zayas cofounded and managed the Modern Art Gallery, initially a branch of 291, which opened in October 1915 with paintings by Picabia, Braque, and Picasso, African sculpture, and photographs by Stieglitz.

Picabia's mechanistic paintings were first featured at the Modern Gallery early in 1916. Shortly thereafter, in April, Schamberg was hailed as "a doughty follower" of Picabia for his five paintings described as "mechanical drawing allegories," on view in a group show at the Bourgeois Gallery, New York.[9] Yet Schamberg was recognized soon after his premature death, in 1918, as something more than a mere protégé. He generally avoided the sense of cryptic irony exploited by Duchamp and Picabia, and his fully developed Precisionist style was, according to Walter Pach, based on his firsthand appreciation of machines. According to Agee, Schamberg distilled his diagrammatic images from such machines as the automatic mixer and the bookbinding wire-stitcher (plates 39–41).[10]

3. Albert Gleizes. *Brooklyn Bridge*. 1915. Oil and gouache on canvas, 40⅛ x 40⅛". Solomon R. Guggenheim Museum, New York, FN 44.942

While Duchamp and Picabia provided the lead for the exploration of machine imagery, Albert Gleizes encouraged the appreciation of New York's skyscrapers and bridges, "as admirable as the most celebrated cathedrals."[11] The dynamic Cubo-Futurist paintings of the Brooklyn Bridge Gleizes painted in 1915–17 (fig. 3) had an impact upon the iconic, exultant rendition of the same subject by his friend Joseph Stella in about 1919 (Yale University Art Gallery).

Whereas Gleizes and Stella expressed their emotional captivation with this urban landmark, Preston Dickinson developed a more sober, objective, proto-Precisionist approach in his early views of High Bridge, the Harlem River, and Fort George Hill in upper Manhattan. Created after his trip to Europe, where he befriended Demuth, these paintings of 1915 combine elements of the work of Giotto and Cézanne, Synthetic Cubism, folk art, and Japanese ukiyo-e prints to emphasize the crisp geometry of the urban landscape. In April 1917, Dickinson was credited with combining "technical precision and intellectual force to a degree hardly approached by any of his companions" in paintings shown at the Daniel Gallery.[12]

The flat, hard-edged planes of Synthetic Cubism also contributed to the early Precisionist styles of Demuth and Sheeler in 1917, which were based on architectural subjects. As early as February of that year, Sheeler was praised for the "clear precision" of his "severely ascetic" drawings of unidentified subjects on view at the Montross Gallery, New York.[13] This description would certainly apply to the series based on the barns of Bucks County, Pennsylvania, which Sheeler first portrayed in his photographs. Exploring the countryside near his rented eighteenth-century fieldstone farmhouse in Doylestown, Sheeler created the pure, planar *Barn Abstraction*, 1917, acquired by the Arensbergs and hung with Schamberg's *Mechanical Abstraction*. He thus inaugurated one of the most significant aspects of Precisionism, the merging of functional, vernacular architecture and artifacts with a modernist vocabulary (plates 107, 110, 112–115, 117).[14]

Demuth's interest in vernacular architecture was nurtured by his lifelong residence in Lancaster, Pennsylvania, in an eighteenth-century home decorated with antiques and modern art. As Betsy Fahlman has observed, the "clean lines of the older buildings and industrial architecture of his native city exerted a strong visual impact on Demuth that remained fundamental to his vision even when he did work elsewhere, such as Bermuda, Gloucester [Massachusetts], or Provincetown [Massachusetts]."[15] During a trip to Bermuda in February–March 1917, Demuth extended the experiments he had begun in 1916 in Provincetown under the influence of the Synthetic Cubist abstractions of nautical motifs by his friend Marsden Hartley. Demuth developed his own personal variant of Cubism (more nuanced and lyrical than Sheeler's), in which the delicately colored, ruler-drawn sharp angles and flat planes of Bermuda's colonial architecture are integrated with the sensuous curves of neighboring trees, in a manner evoking Cézanne's late watercolors (plates 109, 111). While in Bermuda, Demuth was also in contact with Gleizes, whose paintings and ideas most likely encouraged his partial shift away from vaudevillian and literary themes to a more austere, abstract, architectonic style.[16]

Gleizes provided an important commentary on contemporary American art in the 1919 catalogue for the Bourgeois Gallery's annual exhibition of international modern art: "It reflects all the tendencies, all the schools, all the shadings; . . . and it is precisely its strength, this leap headforemost into the *impersonal. . . .*"[17] For Sheeler, the impersonal was a key aspect of a classical, structural approach, as opposed to the seemingly formless romanticism of his teacher Chase and the Impressionists. Thus the critical and stylistic evolution of Precisionism must be situated within the international context of the classicizing, constructive, machine age "call to order" movements, evolving after the chaos and destruction of World War I. Critics of this period frequently employed the term "precision" to characterize not only the clean, economic lines of machinery and of classical and vernacular architecture, but also the precise definition of forms in the work of artists as diverse as Sheeler, Lozowick, and Demuth.

4. Le Corbusier (Charles-Édouard Jeanneret). *Still Life*. 1920. Oil on canvas, 31⅞ x 39¼". The Museum of Modern Art, New York. Van Gogh Purchase Fund

PRECISIONISM, CLASSICISM, THE MACHINE AESTHETIC, AND THE VERNACULAR TRADITION

In a May 1919 review of Schamberg's memorial exhibition, the astute critic Henry McBride concluded that the artist "would surely have been an important figure in the new life that is beginning to find expression."[18] He then quoted extensively from *Après le Cubisme* (After Cubism) by Amédée Ozenfant and Charles-Édouard Jeanneret, better known as Le Corbusier, the architect and painter. Published in November 1918 in Paris, *Après le Cubisme* was the manifesto of the movement known as Purism. In it the authors proposed a purified art based on strict, rational laws of composition and form to convey a new world order. Their own paintings of manufactured still-life subjects in muted colors were based on a simplified Cubism, executed in a more severe, mechanical manner than Picasso's and Braque's (fig. 4). Ozenfant and Le Corbusier equated a return to the eternal, classical principles of structure and form with the purity and geometry of mechanical forms, ancient and primitive art, the work of Cézanne, Seurat, and such contemporary artists as Picasso, Léger, Gris, Braque, and Derain. In one of their most important articles on the formation of a modern way of seeing, they referred to the "innumerable objects of modern industry, all characterized by this imperative precision."[19] In his landmark book *Vers une Architecture* of 1923 (published in 1927 as *Towards a New Architecture*), Le Corbusier frequently employed the term "precision" to relate the grandeur of modern machinery and factories (especially those of America) to classical, ancient architecture.

At home, several American publications and critics promoted the machine aesthetic as the basis for a vital, native art—notably Robert Coady's magazine *The Soil* (1916–17), Matthew Josephson's *Broom* (1921–24), and Jane Heap's *The Little Review* (1914–29). In *Broom*, Bernard De Fayet observed, "Our epoch . . . has its spirit—Great industry, great finance, great administration; a spirit made of love of precision, objectivity and calculation, a noticeable refinement of everything, a need of order, of abstraction. . . . Our epoch demands a proud and simple art. . . ."[20] Critic and historian Lewis Mumford in 1922 proclaimed the "promise of a stripped, athletic, classical style . . . which shall embody all that is good in the Machine Age: its precision, its cleanliness, its hard illumination, its unflinching logic."[21]

One of the leading Precisionists Mumford admired was Louis Lozowick, a regular contributor to *Broom* and *The Little Review* who traveled to Paris, Berlin, and Moscow in 1920–24. The following year saw the publication of his pioneering monograph on modern Russian art, in which he concluded, "[Artists should not] copy the machine [but] build [their] own work with the same precision of clearly defined forms . . . the same economy in the choice of means. . . ."[22]

In Paris, Lozowick had met Léger, who credited architects and film directors with creating the new taste "for simplicity . . . precision . . . architectural clarity."[23] He extolled the beauty of machines and manufactured objects in articles published in *The Little Review* and designed the cover for the catalogue of the international Machine Age Exposition of May 1927. Duchamp and several of the Precisionists—Lozowick, Sheeler, Demuth, and Ralph Steiner—were involved with the organization of this landmark show, which juxtaposed examples of modern art, architectural renderings, photographs of contemporary office and factory buildings, and a wide range of mechanical objects. Lozowick's substantial essay for the catalogue is often quoted as a manifesto for Precisionism as a machine aesthetic (see Appendix).

The first exhibition in New York to group modern art with machinery as "precise" objects of beauty had been organized by the independent, jury-free Salons of America in May 1923. American ship models, African and native North and South American art, Gothic sculpture, Egyptian and Greek art, works by Picasso, and mechanical objects were featured, along with the work of what McBride called the "Be Hard School": Sheeler's photograph of a Pennsylvania barn, Edward Bruce's painting of the "implacable New Yorkscrapers,"[24] and George Ault's *Millroom* of 1923 (Fine Arts Museums of San Francisco), inspired by his experiences at his father's ink plant.

Mumford believed that there was "nothing peculiar to machine-technology" in its virtues of "precision, economy, finish, geometric perfection," observing that "the modern factory shares them with the old New England mill, the modern grain elevator with the Pennsylvania barn, the steamship with the clipper."[25] He and others established affinities between America's earlier vernacular traditions and the machine age at a time of growing interest in the country's fine and folk art heritage. In 1923, the term "skyscraper primitive" was coined to characterize the artistic pioneers who celebrated American technology. All of these phenomena were central to a pervasive search for national identity in the arts and culture.[26]

Among the first to appreciate the folk art of the "American primitives" were the Precisionists Niles Spencer, Stefan Hirsch, and Ault. They "got the folk art fever" from Hamilton Easter Field and his summer art colony in Ogunquit, Maine, which featured studios constructed out of old barns to conform with the vernacular simplicity of neighboring fishing huts.[27] The first significant exhibition of early American paintings, prints, carvings, and decorative art was presented by Gertrude Vanderbilt Whitney's Studio Club in New York in 1924. Among the lenders to this show was Demuth, as well as Sheeler, whose two early American portraits were characterized as "amazingly up-to-date" with "the austerity and simplicity of Derain or a Picasso."[28]

During the 1920s, the Whitney Studio Club and the Daniel Gallery, also in New York, were the major showcases for most of the Precisionists. In order to elucidate the origins and meaning of the term "Precisionist" in relation to these artists, it is interesting to sample the criticism of their solo and group shows at these and other galleries.

THE DEVELOPMENT OF PRECISIONISM DURING THE 1920S

By 1920, Charles Daniel had emerged as the most consistent supporter of the artists who would come to be known as the Precisionists. A former saloonkeeper whose pioneering role has been eclipsed by that of Alfred Stieglitz, Daniel was credited in his time with "an enviable record of long and single combat for the welfare of the unrecognized genius treading new paths."[29] He regularly featured the work of Demuth, Dickinson, Sheeler, and Spencer, as well as the younger artists Henry Billings, Peter Blume, Elsie Driggs, and Charles Goeller, until 1932. By the end of the 1920s, critics referred to these artists as Precisionists and, more commonly, as members of the Immaculate School. They discussed the range of Precisionist work in stylistically coherent terms, perceiving such common denominators as precision, objectivity, simplification, and architectonic structure—the hallmarks of a highly refined, selective realism.

By 1922, the gallery's reputation for showing the "most intellectual art of its sort" was commented upon by reviewers.[30] Contributing to this status was

5. Charles Sheeler. *Church Street El.* 1920. Oil on canvas, 16⅛ x 19⅛". The Cleveland Museum of Art, Ohio. Mr. and Mrs. William H. Marlatt Fund, 77.43

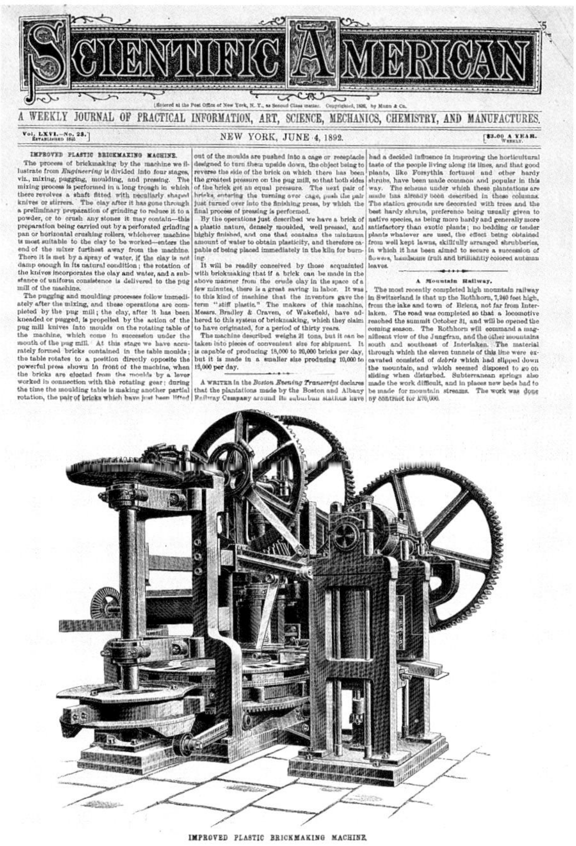

SCIENTIFIC AMERICAN

[Entered at the Post Office of New York, N. Y., as Second Class matter. Copyrighted, 1892, by Munn & Co.

A WEEKLY JOURNAL OF PRACTICAL INFORMATION, ART, SCIENCE, MECHANICS, CHEMISTRY, AND MANUFACTURES.

Vol. LXVI.—No. 23.] ESTABLISHED 1845 | NEW YORK, JUNE 4, 1892. | [$3.00 A YEAR. WEEKLY.

IMPROVED PLASTIC BRICKMAKING MACHINE.

The process of brickmaking by the machine we illustrate from *Engineering* is divided into four stages, viz., mixing, pugging, moulding, and pressing. The mixing process is performed in a long trough in which there revolves a shaft fitted with peculiarly shaped knives or stirrers. The clay after it has gone through a preliminary preparation of grinding to reduce it to a powder, or to crush any stones it may contain—this preparation being carried out by a perforated grinding pan or horizontal crushing rollers, whichever machine is most suitable to the clay to be worked—enters the end of the mixer furthest away from the machine. There it is met by a spray of water, if the clay is not damp enough in its natural condition; the rotation of the knives incorporates the clay and water, and a substance of uniform consistence is delivered to the pug mill of the machine.

The pugging and moulding processes follow immediately after the mixing, and these operations are completed by the pug mill; the clay, after it has been kneaded or pugged, is propelled by the action of the pug mill knives into moulds on the rotating table of the machine, which come in succession under the mouth of the pug mill. At this stage we have accurately formed bricks contained in the table moulds; the table rotates to a position directly opposite the powerful press shown in front of the machine, when the bricks are ejected from the moulds by a lever worked in connection with the rotating gear; during the time the moulding table is making another partial rotation, the pair of bricks which have just been lifted out of the moulds are pushed into a cage or receptacle designed to turn them upside down, the object being to reverse the side of the brick on which there has been the greatest pressure on the pug mill, so that both sides of the brick get an equal pressure. The next pair of bricks, entering the turning over cage, push the pair just turned over into the finishing press, by which the final process of pressing is performed.

By the operations just described we have a brick of a plastic nature, densely moulded, well pressed, and highly finished, and one that contains the minimum amount of water to obtain plasticity, and therefore capable of being placed immediately in the kiln for burning.

It will be readily conceived by those acquainted with brickmaking that if a brick can be made in the above manner from the crude clay in the space of a few minutes, there is a great saving in labor. It was to this kind of machine that the inventors gave the term "stiff plastic." The makers of this machine, Messrs. Bradley & Craven, of Wakefield, have adhered to this system of brickmaking, which they claim to have originated, for a period of thirty years.

The machine described weighs 21 tons, but it can be taken into pieces of convenient size for shipment. It is capable of producing 18,000 to 20,000 bricks per day, but it is made in a smaller size producing 10,000 to 12,000 per day.

A WRITER in the *Boston Evening Transcript* declares that the plantations made by the Boston and Albany Railway Company around its suburban stations have had a decided influence in improving the horticultural taste of the people living along its lines, and that good plants, like Forsythia fortunei and other hardy shrubs, have been made common and popular in this way. The scheme under which these plantations are made has already been described in these columns. The station grounds are decorated with trees and the best hardy shrubs, preference being usually given to native species, as being more hardy and generally more satisfactory than exotic plants; no bedding or tender plants whatever are used, the effect being obtained from well kept lawns, skillfully arranged shrubberies, in which it has been aimed to secure a succession of flowers, handsome fruit and brilliantly colored autumn leaves.

A Mountain Railway.

The most recently completed high mountain railway in Switzerland is that up the Rothhorn, 7,240 feet high, from the lake and town of Brienz, not far from Interlaken. The road was completed so that a locomotive reached the summit October 31, and will be opened the coming season. The Rothhorn will command a magnificent view of the Jungfrau, and the other mountains south and southeast of Interlaken. The material through which the eleven tunnels of this line were excavated consisted of *debris* which had slipped down the mountain, and which seemed disposed to go on sliding when disturbed. Subterranean springs also made the work difficult, and in places new beds had to be made for mountain streams. The work was done by contract for £70,000.

IMPROVED PLASTIC BRICKMAKING MACHINE.

6. "Improved Plastic Brickmaking Machine." *Scientific American*, vol. 66, June 4, 1892, p. 349. Science and Technology Research Center, The New York Public Library, Astor, Lenox, and Tilden Foundations

Demuth, whose "sane, impersonal" paintings of New England churches and Pennsylvania industry (plate 45) were praised in 1920 for their "exquisite precision."[31] In 1922, Sheeler's first one-man show at the Daniel Gallery featured still lifes and "views of skyscrapers, painted in flat tones and angular in pattern" noted for their "linear precision."[32] He achieved what one critic later called "the requisite precision and impersonality" in his dehumanized treatment of New York's "prevailing geometric forms . . . ideally suited to the simplifications of modern art"[33] (fig. 5, plate 12).

In 1923 and 1924, the Belmaison Galleries organized comprehensive exhibitions surveying the history of New York in art. Included were historical prints related to an objective tradition of late nineteenth-century magazine illustrations of mechanical objects, factories, and city views (fig. 6), which have been studied as prototypes for similar Precisionist subjects.[34] Also featured were painterly, humanist works by the Ashcan School urban realists Robert Henri, John Sloan, and George Bellows, as well as the "visionary ecstasies" of Abraham Walkowitz, who, along with John Marin (fig. 7) and Max Weber, conveyed the prewar dynamism of New York's skyline in an expressively fragmented, Cubo-Futurist style.[35] Finally, the youngest generation, including Sheeler, Stella, Spencer, Ault, Dickinson, and Hirsch, was char-

7. John Marin. *St. Paul's, Manhattan.* 1914. Watercolor on paper, 15⅞ x 18⅞". The Metropolitan Museum of Art, New York. The Alfred Stieglitz Collection, 1949, 49.70.110

acterized as having "avoided the atmospheric effects of New York. . . . so violent and universal is the reaction [against] impressionism [in favor of] design"[36] (plate 13).

Although Demuth did not paint views of New York, he had cemented his pioneering status as a distinctive painter of industrial America with his shows in late 1922 and 1923 at the Daniel Gallery. Credited with an elusive Duchampian sense of humor and an ability to convey the beauty of precise industrial forms, Demuth was regarded as a quintessentially American modernist with a "method almost scientific in its precision . . . its refinement, its reticence, its disdain of all that is heavy-handed . . . in tune with everything that has hitherto been finest in American art."[37]

In 1923 and 1924, Dickinson's work was featured in solo and group exhibitions at the Daniel Gallery. His still lifes, drawings of the High Bridge, and other urban and industrial views (plates 10, 11, 51, 90) were repeatedly praised for their grace, precision, elegance, and "architectural relation."[38] The term "immaculate" was used in 1923 to describe the condition of the factory roofs in Dickinson's *Industry* (plate 50), "a composition that is quite literal though expounded with abstract form."[39] Soon thereafter, critics began calling Dickinson and other Daniel Gallery painters the "Immaculates," referring to the clean lines of the machines they depicted as well as to the machines' beneficent potential to promote universal hygiene.[40]

In reviews of Daniel group shows in 1924, Spencer was praised for the "sincerity and strength" of his "somber . . . cubistic" landscapes, painted "with a satisfying cleanliness that makes one realize . . . why that virtue is allotted so important a place."[41] Similarly, Georgia O'Keeffe was repeatedly praised for the cleanness and purity of her technique, evident in the paintings of still lifes, flowers, and landscapes exhibited at Anderson Galleries, New York, in 1923 and 1924. Although O'Keeffe's subjects were not machine-age products, Paul Rosenfeld observed that much "of her work has the precision of the most finely machine-cut products."[42]

The forms of O'Keeffe's paintings were also described as being "suspended in a vacuum undisturbed by variations of light and atmosphere."[43] Sheeler similarly characterized "his effort 'to suspend the forms in a vacuum'" in order "to eliminate the interception of the medium between the eyes of the spectator and the creation of the artist."[44] Virgil Barker tried to distinguish between the two artists' work with the following often quoted remark: "O'Keeffe's pictures are the clean-cut result of an intensely passionate apprehension of things; Mr. Sheeler's, the clean-cut result of an apprehension that is intensely intellectual."[45]

Sheeler stressed his preference for the cerebral aspects of art through his selection of works by Duchamp, Picasso, Braque, and de Zayas for exhibition at the Whitney Studio Club in March 1924; these examples were characterized by reviewers as "severely intellectual abstractions" possessing "the air of classics."[46] His own art (primarily still lifes), shown there later that month, was described in similar terms: "Selection, elimination and intention are the inherent qualities of Mr. Sheeler's intellectual art, even as precision and control are its outward manifestations."[47] Sheeler's profound understanding of Cubism is evident in his *Still Life and Shadows* (plate 93). By adopting his photographic technique of lighting a subject from varied angles, Sheeler created intersecting planes that do not, however, disrupt the integrity of the early American objects on the table.

The critic Forbes Watson detected the "American root of Sheeler's art" in "the clean-cut fineness, the cool austerity, the complete distrust of superfluities which we find in some pieces of early American furniture."[48] Although the Whitney Studio Club represented a wide range of styles, many of the artists later known as Immaculates or Precisionists were featured in annual, group, or solo shows: Ault, Billings, Davis, Demuth, Driggs, Dickinson, Spencer, Stella, Earl Horter, and Lozowick. A smaller group than the large, jury-free Society of Independents and Salons of America, the Club could serve as a barometer for tendencies in contemporary art. In 1926, Club members Spencer, Dickinson, and Sheeler were grouped together for striking an "American note" which "is there to a marked degree in the precision and craftsmanship" of their paintings.[49]

In 1925, Spencer, a slow, methodical painter like many of his Precisionist colleagues, had finally produced enough works for his first one-man show at the Daniel Gallery. A devotee of Giotto and Cézanne, Spencer painted his seemingly plain yet distinctively textured architectural landscapes in Ogunquit and Provincetown; he was praised for these and his "aristocratic, detached" still lifes (plates 95, 118, 119).[50] Henry McBride observed that "Mr. Spencer is one of those who sees cubism in nature and since he gets it direct from Her, it would be equally correct to dub him a realist."[51] He called this "après-cubisme work," referring to Ozenfant and Le Corbusier's manifesto of Purism. Spencer's work was also included in a group show at America's first museum of modern art, the Phillips Memorial Art Gallery in Washington, D.C., in January 1926. This significant exhibition marked the beginning of a growing recognition of Precisionist directions in American art, not only by dealers but also museum professionals and members of academia.

Planning a series of shows on contemporary trends, museum founder and director Duncan Phillips grouped the architectural paintings of Spencer, Dickinson, Hirsch, Demuth, Sheeler, and others, to demonstrate that "drastic modifications of the Cult of Cubism are being made in America."[52] He observed that Sheeler "believes painters should not neglect mechanical means to interpret a mechanical age. To express the impersonal character of his epoch he . . . reduces to the bare elements of design what he sees or photographs with his sharp lens. . . . Sheeler's work is clean, deft, and drastic like that of a skillful surgeon."[53]

Robert Allerton Parker employed the same scientific metaphors in a major article on Sheeler in May 1926: "Charles Sheeler seeks to disengage, with a precision that . . . seems almost surgical, the essential forms of his object from all the mere vicissitudes through which it has lived."[54] Discussing Sheeler's ability to define objects "with a precision that is almost Euclidean," Parker related his skills to the "miraculous conquests of modern science . . . due to . . . the remarkable refinement of its instruments of precision."[55] He also observed that criticism of Sheeler's work as "too 'immaculate,' too precious, even too pedantic . . . is based upon a fundamental misunderstanding of the [artist's] aim . . . [to perpetuate] the classic tradition . . . of the Greeks, of Giotto, Mantegna, and of Ingres."[56] Among the critics who characterized Sheeler's art as too "immaculate" were the editors of *Art News*, Guy Eglington and Deoch Fulton. On January 23, 1926, they published what may be the first article to refer to the "Immaculate School."

In a review of Sheeler's 1926 show at J.B. Neumann's New Art Circle in New York, his "process of refinement" was defined as a reaction: "Against the slaughter-house tradition of Chase, developed by Bellows to massacre pitch . . . the Immaculate School opposed fineness of vision, clarity and exactitude of statement."[57]

Given that Lozowick's paintings and drawings of urban and technological subjects were on view at the New Art Circle at the same time as Sheeler's, the two artists probably became acquainted at this time. Lozowick may have served Sheeler and others as a key source of information on related artistic developments in Europe such as Purism, Constructivism, the Bauhaus, and the New Objectivity movement. Although this was his first American one-man show, Lozowick was already known in 1924 for the "pure flat colors," reductive, "severely architectural forms," and rhythmic "precision" of his paintings of American cities (plates 15, 21).[58] Acutely aware of European enthusiasm for American technology, Lozowick executed the City series incorporating Cubist, Futurist, and Constructivist elements. When exhibited in Berlin in 1923, they were praised for their "American vigor and precision."[59]

In his one-man show at the New Art Circle, Lozowick's City paintings were accompanied by his refined, semiabstract drawings based on sections of machinery—the Machine Ornaments (plate 61), which provided the foundation for his applied design work. One reviewer contrasted Lozowick with Joseph Stella and his vision of technology: "Stella sees the chaotic confusion of the machine age, Lozowick sees its essential orderliness, its integration."[60]

Similarly, Joseph Stella's monumental *The Voice of the City of New York Interpreted* (fig. 8) was described as "one of the earlier landmarks of modern art in America" when it was exhibited in his one-man show of April 1926: "Since the New York set was painted, a process of clarification has been taking place, so that were . . . anyone . . . to undertake such a service again their achievement would present a severer and more unified appearance. . . . For a moment of stabilization

8. Joseph Stella. *The Voice of the City of New York Interpreted.* 1920–22. Oil and tempera on canvas, five panels; *The Skyscrapers* 99¾ x 54", other four 88½ x 54". Collection The Newark Museum. Purchase, Felix Fuld Bequest Fund, 1937, 37.288

This complex, monumental homage to New York consists of five canvases: *The Port (The Harbor, The Battery), The White Way I, The Skyscrapers (The Prow), The White Way II (Broadway),* and *The Bridge (Brooklyn Bridge).*

is on us, which . . . may well come to be regarded as a classic era."[61] Some of Stella's urban and industrial scenes can be called Precisionist, in terms of their sharply defined, static, simplified forms (fig. 9, plates 43, 44). His romantic, poetic sensibility, however, usually resulted in works that do not fit comfortably within this category.

Another of the Precisionists who often defied categorization was Demuth, who also had a one-man show in 1926. Despite his range and complexity, some critics continued to cast him in the Precisionist role. In a Daniel Gallery group show, his floral watercolors were praised—in terms similar to those describing Sheeler's work—for their "careful arrangement, the nothing in excess, and the cool refinement," as well as "the cleanest and purest [colors] in the world."[62]

By early 1927, Sheeler was established as the influential head of the "Immaculate School," at least in the eyes of *Art News*. In a review of her solo show at Daniel Gallery, Katherine Schmidt was characterized as having "developed her [smooth] brushwork according to the Sheeleresque Immaculate school [which] forces one to admire the representative qualities in her painting and her photographic eye."[63] Other artists, like the Expressionist Karl Knaths, with his capricious, "seemingly casual arrangements," were considered to be "at war with the 'immaculate

9. Joseph Stella. *By-Products Storage Tanks*. ca. 1920. Charcoal on paper, 21 7/8 x 28". Santa Barbara Museum of Art. Gift of Wright S. Ludington

painters' who hold the fort at Daniel's."[64] Indeed Duncan Phillips admonished Daniel, "Dont [sic] edit Knaths too much nor try to make as cold and intellectual a craftsman as some of your other men."[65]

Similar observations regarding the cool, intellectual nature of O'Keeffe's work were made at the time of her solo show at the Intimate Gallery, New York, in January 1927. Referring to O'Keeffe's new paintings of the Shelton Hotel, McBride observed, "It is not emotional work because the processes are concealed. . . . Emotion would not permit such plodding precision."[66] Between 1925 and 1930, O'Keeffe painted over twenty New York scenes; some are placid vistas from her windows and others are awe-inspiring views of towers seen from street level (plates 23, 24). She continued to paint her trademark flowers (plate 106), later recalling that she made "them big like the huge buildings going up" in New York so "they'll *have* to look at them."[67]

From an apartment window, Elsie Driggs painted *Queensborough Bridge* (plate 22) in 1927, possibly aware of the precedent set by Joseph Stella's renowned *Brooklyn Bridge*. Well received in a Daniel Gallery group show in April, Driggs's depiction of the Queensborough Bridge and its neighboring smokestack was described as "a clear and cerebral impression of the well-known structure, recognizing the rigid lines of the metal work but softening them with planes of light, and achieving good decoration."[68] Prior to this show, since her gallery debut in 1924, Driggs was known for her drawings of flowers and vegetables, which were compared to Demuth's in terms of their forceful delicacy and austerity.

Driggs was also represented earlier in 1927 in the Whitney Studio Club's annual exhibition, along with Dickinson and Spencer. The latter two were characterized in a review by the critic Louis Kalonyme as the leading "precisionists"—perhaps the earliest use of this label. According to Kalonyme, they had a tendency to oversimplify forms: "Leon Hartl's 'American Window' proves that a composition can be precise without being toylike—something neither of our two foremost precisionists, Preston Dickinson and Niles Spencer, can quite prove in their own work."[69]

It is difficult to ascertain how common the official use of the term "Precisionist" was at this point. The artists at the Daniel Gallery were established by *Art News* as the "Immaculate School"; however, Charles Daniel called them the "New Classicists." Elsie Driggs has recalled Daniel's inclusion of her in this group of artists at his gallery. Similarly, Peter Blume, who had his debut there in 1926, has recollected that Daniel's associate, the poet Alanson Hartpence, was the gallery's intellectual force and frequently discussed "the antithesis of classical and romantic" as "the emphasis on form rather than subject matter and . . . personal expression."[70] Both Daniel and Hartpence may have had an impact upon Alfred H. Barr Jr., who, as Associate Professor at Wellesley College, borrowed works from the gallery for his exhibition *Progressive Modern Painting* at Wellesley in April 1927. In it, Barr identified four postwar art movements, grouping Sheeler and Dickinson under the category of the Neoclassicists.

Barr taught the first comprehensive course in modern art at any American college and had a scholarly penchant for classification that resulted in what may be the first official use of the term "Precisionist" in May 1927. At that time, Barr lectured on the topic "Tendencies in Modern American Painting" at the

Institute of Art, Bowdoin College. Having asked many artists and critics to name the "most conspicuous characteristic of American painting," Barr contented himself with illustrating "certain important tendencies" using slides of work by, among others, "the Precisionists . . . Charles Sheeler and Charles Demuth."[71]

Nevertheless, the term "Immaculate School" continued to dominate the criticism and was extended in 1928 to encompass several painters other than those exhibiting at the Daniel Gallery, including Hirsch and Ault, who showed at the Downtown Gallery, New York. Founded in 1926 and directed by Edith Halpert, the Downtown Gallery became the major showcase for artists working in Precisionist styles, especially after the closing of the Daniel Gallery in 1932. In a group exhibition of "modernistic blossoms" in May 1928, Hirsch's *Lilies of the Valley* was described as being "a little afflicted with the anemia of the immaculate school."[72]

Late in 1928, Ault had a one-man show at Downtown, which included *From Brooklyn Heights*, an awesome view of smoke-spewing waterfront industry and an oceanliner, with New York's massive skyline in the background. The eerie ambiance of this work and others has been linked to the influence of Surrealism, as well as Ault's emotional unrest, and growing terror of New York, with its skyscraper "tombstones of capitalism"—all of which belie his later neutral "precisionist" statement about this picture[73] (plate 16). In reviews, Ault was praised as "an excellent draughtsman, somewhat inclined towards the immaculate school" and as having "a decided flair for the abstract, building up his design in somber tones with architectural precision of structure. . . . [and] subtle color relations."[74]

Coinciding with Ault's show was a group exhibition at the Daniel Gallery that would prove to be a key event in defining Precisionism. In an unsigned review entitled "Immaculate School Seen at Daniel's," the following terse, often-quoted statement summarized the characteristics of the style, in terms of a machine aesthetic, linked to urban-industrial subjects: "Factories, sheds, bridges, and smokestacks loom large in the current Daniel showing, all rendered in the precise line, flat color, and clearly defined pattern that have become trademarks of the immaculate school."[75] For Edward Alden Jewell, the Daniel Gallery exhibition provided an opportunity to "begin to see more clearly one at least of the main directions that modern art . . . is taking" in America: "This art is architectural, precise, dealing . . . in large, fairly simple surfaces drawn into relationship through weighing, sifting, and digesting some of the salient experimental processes of the past. Cubism played its part, though it does not anywhere survive as such. Simplification looms, without erasing all save the grin of the Cheshire cat."[76]

Jewell's subsequent discussion of the architectural direction evident in paintings depicting a range of subjects was remarkably in accordance with Sheeler's later analysis of his own work: "For I would arrive at the picture . . . through a conception of form architectural in its structure, whether flowers or buildings are the theme, set forth with the utmost clarity by means of craftsmanship so adequate as to be unobtrusive."[77]

Represented in the 1928 Daniel Gallery show by an interior still-life study, Sheeler had already begun to explore in photographs and works on paper the industrial subject for which he would become famous, the Ford Motor Company's River Rouge plant (plates 54–57). Therefore, he probably paid close attention to Elsie Driggs's acclaimed painting in the Daniel Gallery show of the smokestacks of the Jones and Laughlin steel mills, *Pittsburgh* (plate 54). Shortly after Sheeler began photographing the River Rouge plant in October 1927 for the Philadelphia advertising firm N.W. Ayer and Son, Driggs made a trip on her own initiative to Pittsburgh. Finding that the steel industry had discontinued the Bessemer process that produced the shooting flames she had admired as a child, Driggs was surprised by the "cool . . . classical" beauty of the mill's smokestacks: "the same laws of proportion . . . [as those] laid down for the proportions of the Greek column."[78] Having traveled to Italy in the company of Leo Stein and fallen in love with the Renaissance masters, Driggs called *Pittsburgh* her "Piero della Francesca."

O'Keeffe continued to paint New York City scenes, and they were included in her Intimate Gallery shows of 1928 and 1929, along with paintings of flowers, fruit, landscapes, still lifes, and abstractions. At this time she painted her last major work on the subject, *New York Night*, a breathtaking view from her window in the Shelton Hotel (plate 24). In it, O'Keeffe created a sense of decorative order and mystery out of the patterns of electrically lit windows and traffic, combined with the cavernous perspective of Lexington Avenue. In May 1929, she was officially grouped, along with Sheeler and Demuth, as a Precisionist in a lecture given by Barr at Wellesley College.

During April and May 1929, Barr gave a lecture series on international modern art that was separate from his regular course on the subject. On May 1, he discussed "Modern American Painting: A Cross-Section," with "The Precisionists" as a distinct group: "In contrast to the work of the Precisionists such as Georgia O'Keeffe, Scheeler [sic], Demuth, and Schmidt, who painted the objective world in simplified masses with strong emphasis on the plastic effect of the color surface, John Marin turned to water-colors and painted instantaneous, directly transferred emotions which the outer world aroused in him."[79] This general, formalistic description is one of the first official statements identifying the Precisionists as a significant group within the eclectic contemporary art scene in America.

Nevertheless, the term "immaculate" remained the more commonly used designation, especially for the Daniel Gallery group. In March 1929, for example, Charles Goeller, a newcomer and friend of Elsie Driggs, was credited with producing an objective, realistic, somewhat cold still-life painting "to challenge any of the 'immaculates.' "[80] Later that year, he was "already quite within the Daniel Gallery tradition," as was another relatively new member, Henry Billings.[81] The latter was grouped with Sheeler, Spencer, and Dickinson for painting "with precision and elegance . . . seem[ing] to know definitely what they are about before they touch brush to canvas"[82] (plate 60).

Early in 1929, Sheeler completed his first oil painting in two years, *Upper Deck* (fig. 10), which paved the way for his River Rouge works of the following year. According to the artist, *Upper Deck*—closely based on a commissioned photograph of the German ocean liner S.S. *Majestic*—represented a major step toward achieving greater objectivity and precision in his art: "It was the first of a group of pictures which was to be still further intent upon precision of construction and execution . . . which would further remove the evidence of painting. . . . Not to produce a replica of nature but to attain an intensified presentation of its essentials, through greater compactness of its formal design by precision of vision and hand, is my objective."[83]

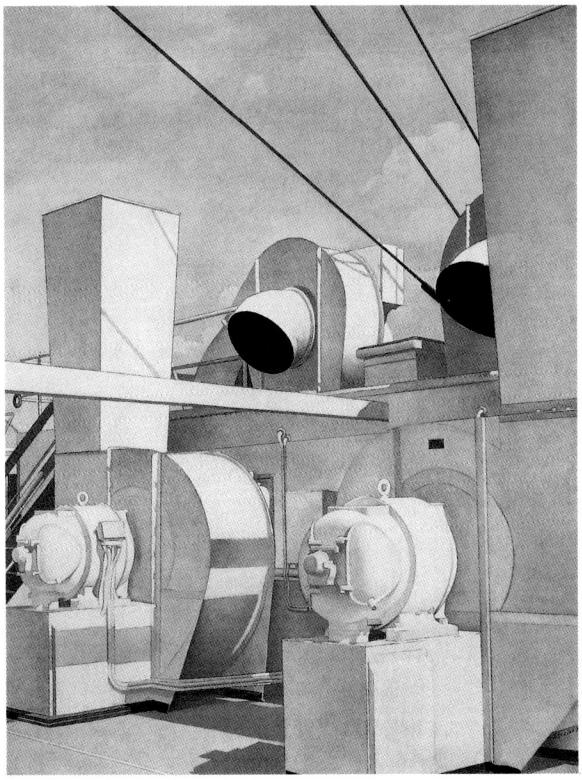

10. Charles Sheeler. *Upper Deck*. 1929. Oil on canvas, 29¼ x 22½". Fogg Art Museum, Harvard University Art Museums, Cambridge, Massachusetts. Louise E. Bettens Fund

Upper Deck was Sheeler's first completely preplanned painting. He based it on a gradually developed mental image, "much as the architect completes his plans before the work of bringing the house into existence begins."[84] The time spent working on *Upper Deck* and subsequent paintings "was [therefore] not consumed by an elaborate technical process of underpainting and glazing, but rather in maintaining precision of statement set down directly with the least possible amount of repainting."[85] *Upper Deck* also confirmed Sheeler's "growing belief that pictures realistically conceived might have an underlying abstract structure."[86] Sheeler's evolving Precisionist aesthetic was reinforced by his 1929 trip to Europe, where he studied the old masters (particularly Holbein and van Eyck) and participated in the major exhibition *Film und Foto* in Stuttgart. There Sheeler probably encountered the New Objectivity movement, with which Barr would publicly identify him in the early 1930s.

PRECISIONISM IN THE 1930S: DISPERSAL, CONSOLIDATION, AND EXPANSION

During the 1930s, Precisionist directions in American art were increasingly varied within the complex Depression-period panorama of the American Scene, Regionalist, and modernist movements. With the closing of the Daniel Gallery in 1932, Halpert's Downtown Gallery became the established showcase well into the 1960s. There, the work of Sheeler, Spencer, O'Keeffe, and newcomer Edmund Lewandowski represented the ongoing vitality of a movement that was abandoned by some (Driggs) or taken in other directions, such as Surrealism (Ault, Hirsch, Francis Criss, Billings, and Blume) and Social Realism (Lozowick, Cook, and Hirsch). Another locus for Precisionism was the art colony in Woodstock, New York, where Billings and Arnold Wiltz were active, as well as Ault, who painted many barns, which he admired for their vernacular simplicity (plate 134). Two of the greatest Precisionist artists—Dickinson and Demuth—were lost as a result of their deaths in 1930 and 1935, respectively.

Some critics, such as Samuel Kootz, viewed Precisionism as an overrefined, inexpressive art that was out of contact with reality. Others, such as Holger Cahill and Edith Halpert, regarded the key figures of Precisionism as contributing still vital, modern expressions of American folk- and fine-art traditions.

The decade opened with Kootz's dire pronouncements in his *Modern American Painters*. For him, Dickinson, "who constructs his pictures in brilliant intellectual order . . . [but] . . . also shares the present American weakness . . . [of] eva[ding] anything too hotly concerned with life," epitomized "all that is good and bad" in native art.[87] Since *Upper Deck*, Sheeler's "new realism. . . . too often tempered by the cameraman's care for detail" had brought him "to the edge of a bloodless and attenuated subterfuge for humanity."[88] In Kootz's opinion, only Demuth—among the older exponents of "our modern classicism . . . able to construct a picture along sound architectural lines"—was able "to attain a more lyric expression" of "individual vitality."[89]

11. Charles Demuth. *Paquebot "Paris."* 1921–22. Oil on canvas, 25 x 20". Columbus Museum of Art, Ohio. Gift of Ferdinand Howald, 1931, 31.139

Among the younger generation, Kootz regarded Blume as "striking out with a zest and driving force that completely dissociate him" from the influence of the " 'Immaculate School' . . . whose refinement is so perilously close to euphuism."[90] He then described Blume's Surrealist tour de force, *Parade*, 1930 (The Museum of Modern Art, New York), which was featured in the artist's first one-man show at Daniel Gallery (as were plates 59, 121). Nevertheless, one reviewer observed that Blume's studies for *Parade* "reveal the infinite patience of the immaculate school."[91] He had incorporated ventilators and other mechanistic imagery into *Parade*, aware of Demuth's pioneering Precisionist depiction of the steamship in *Paquebot "Paris"* (fig. 11) and Sheeler's *Upper Deck*. There may have also been a fruitful exchange of ideas, as indicated by a letter from Daniel to Ferdinand Howald, the Ohio industrialist, leading collector of American modernist art, and major patron of the gallery: "Sheeler is doing better work and we feel he has been helped by Blume. He thought Blume's 'Parade' the high spot of Modern Painting in America."[92] Whether or not Sheeler's new, selective realism was reinforced by his appreciation of Blume's work, the younger artist has recalled a spirit of camaraderie: "When the light failed on winter afternoons the Daniel Gallery painters—and it was a very fine stable indeed, consisting of people like Kuniyoshi, Sheeler, Spencer, Demuth, and Preston Dickinson, among others—would gather in the back room, smoke, and talk and laugh."[93]

In addition to Provincetown, where many of the artists spent their summers, another significant meeting place was the Greenwich Village coffeehouse Romany Marie's, where Blume saw Duchamp (whom he admired), Dickinson, Stuart Davis, and Spencer. Like Driggs, Blume particularly appreciated Spencer's paintings for their Purist clarity. Although Blume rejected the terms "Precisionism" and the "Immaculates," he continued to believe that "there was a homogeneity of style [based on definite line] in the Daniel Gallery, with the exception . . . of Marin."[94]

Until the gallery closed in 1932, Charles Daniel continued to exhibit artists working in Precisionist modes, such as the still-life painter Rosella Hartman. Known for the "architectonic value" of her plant studies exhibited at the Whitney Studio Club in 1930, Hartman was praised for the "extreme simplicity" and "precise . . . line" of her graphic work shown at the Daniel Gallery in late 1931 (plate 101).[95]

With the winding down of the Daniel Gallery's activities in the early 1930s, the Downtown Gallery's exhibitions assumed greater importance as a showcase for Precisionist artists. In March 1931, Demuth and Sheeler, "both artists of marked refinement," exhibited floral watercolors "drawn with great precision and delicacy," providing, along with Dickinson, "the chaste point of view."[96] Stuart Davis, since his first Downtown Gallery exhibition in 1927, had been praised for the "cunning precision" and "severe purity" of his logically arranged compositions in which nonessentials are eliminated.[97] Davis himself had defined his goals in terms that relate to aspects of the Precisionist aesthetic: "A work of art . . . should be impersonal in execution. . . . direct . . . well built. . . . the various planes in perfect balance like a building . . . a simplified statement in paint of the natural objects of great clarity."[98]

Davis is commonly regarded as a unique individual who was the first among the generation of 1930s American modernists to transform his appreciation of the country's industrial, urban, and maritime environments into a consistent, complex, Synthetic Cubist vocabulary of form (fig. 12, plates 94, 120). Although Davis ultimately transcends tidy classification, he was related to the Precisionists by contemporary critics Halpert and Cahill. Halpert remarked in April 1931:

> *He is to my mind the outstanding representative of the so-called abstract school, although his approach is quite different from that of any other member. . . . He makes accurate studies of nature, and uses representational forms, individually definitely recognizable but composed in a very original manner. . . . To me it is almost a logical follow-up of the so-called immaculate school which includes men like Sheeler, Spencer, etc. representing the true American, Puritan art.*[99]

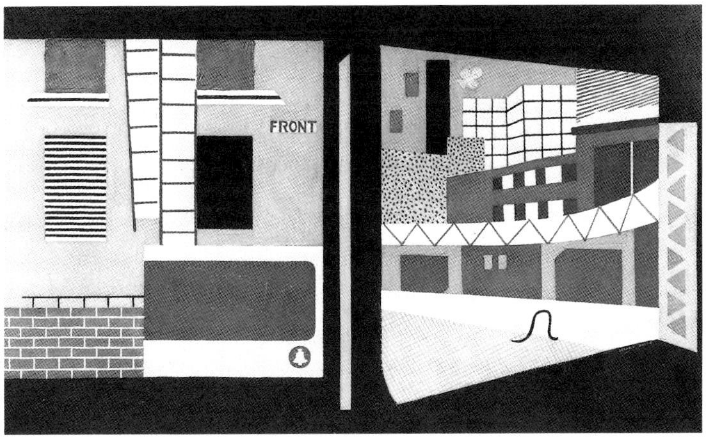

12. Stuart Davis. *House and Street*. 1931. Oil on canvas, 26 × 42¼". Collection Whitney Museum of American Art. Purchase, 41.3

The left half of the picture depicts a facade on Front Street in lower Manhattan; to the right is the track of the Third Avenue Elevated—also visible in Francis Criss's *Third Avenue El* (plate 33).

13. Charles Sheeler. *Home Sweet Home.* 1931. Oil on canvas, 36 x 29¼". The Detroit Institute of Arts. Gift of Robert H. Tannahill

Early in 1931, Barr referred to the work of Sheeler and other Precisionists within the international context of the New Objectivity movement. In his ground-breaking catalogue for the first major survey in America of modern German art, Barr discussed *die Neue Sachlichkeit* as "emphatic and frequently exact realistic painting of the objective world. . . . [with] adherents in other countries . . . in America, . . . Sheeler . . . Hopper, . . . Hirsch, and . . . Schmidt,"[100] He expanded his discussion for a paper delivered at the College Art Association conference, adding Goeller, Hirsch, and Blume to the list of American artists he considered New Objectivists, summarizing their general shift away from Cubist abstraction to selective realism.[101] Another Precisionist associated with the "clarity and . . . architectonic arrangement" of the New Objectivists was Wiltz, a former engineer noted for the "neat precision" of his industrial scenes and Woodstock landscapes (plate 73).[102]

Although Barr and others saw Sheeler and the Precisionists in this international context, Halpert was determined to emphasize his native qualities, observing that "his pictures have the clarity, the purity of form, and the rigid adherence to essentials—characteristic of the American mind."[103]

Halpert's belief in links between America's industrial present and its arts and crafts traditions was shared by Sheeler, who suggested an indigenous craft heritage for American technological enterprise in *Home Sweet Home* (fig. 13), which was featured on the cover of the catalogue to his 1931 Downtown Gallery exhibition. In this painting, based on a comfortable room of his home in South Salem, New York, Sheeler juxtaposed Shaker furniture, rag rugs, a nineteenth-century slat-backed chair, and traditional fireplace with a modern, streamlined oil burner. For Sheeler, the same principles of precision, functional "simplicity of vision, and directness of statement" governed the examples of modern and historical vernacular design that he himself collected.[104]

Also featured in this show were Sheeler's masterful, dehumanized homages to industry, *Classic Landscape* and *American Landscape* (fig. 24, plate 65). Sheeler was later hailed as a "Raphael of the Fords" and "a sort of Fra Angelico [whose] work has the same ascetic, faithful approach to the forms . . . of industrialism, as had the Florentine monk toward the religious imagery of his day."[105]

Sheeler's *Classic Landscape* was one of the important works included in The Museum of Modern Art's major survey of American art from 1862 to 1932, held in 1932. The first of its kind, this exhibition was organized by Halpert's collaborator, Holger Cahill. A pioneering champion of American folk art and modernism, and the future director of the WPA Federal Art Project, Cahill wrote an important catalogue essay with a section devoted to Precisionism, which he characterized in this way: "The modern search for structure is apparent in the work of a group of painters who interpret the American scene with an austere realism, amounting almost to a for-

14. Charles Sheeler. *Americana*. 1931. Oil on canvas, 48 × 36". The Metropolitan Museum of Art, New York. Edith and Milton Lowenthal Collection, Bequest of Edith Abrahamson Lowenthal, 1992.24.8

15. Georgia O'Keeffe. *Lake George Window*. 1929. Oil on canvas, 40 × 30". The Museum of Modern Art, New York. Acquired through the Richard D. Brixey Bequest

mal purism."[106] Cahill regarded Sheeler and Demuth as the group's pioneers, and O'Keeffe as a leading member: "Sheeler is the artist of the mechanical age, interpreting it with an objectivity and a precise spatial arrangement which rules out everything but the sheer elements of design. Demuth . . . has elegance of formal pattern . . . Georgia O'Keeffe articulates her design with great clarity . . . delicacy, and austerity. . . ."[107] He also discussed the work of other members, including Dickinson, Spencer, Hirsch, Blume, and Davis, who "seeks a balance between realistic vision and the methods of abstraction."[108]

Coinciding with Cahill's survey of American art at the Modern was the first Biennial exhibition at the Whitney Museum of American Art. America's first museum devoted solely to progressive native art had opened to great fanfare in November 1931 with an installation that included Dickinson's *Industry* (plate 50), Spencer's *Green Table* (plate 103), Demuth's *My Egypt* (fig. 21), and Driggs's *Pittsburgh* (plate 58). In the 1932 Biennial, the Precisionists dominated the first gallery, with paintings by Ault, Blume, Criss, Demuth, Hirsch, Horter, O'Keeffe, Sheeler, Spencer, and Wiltz. Visual connections between their work were also made in the catalogue; Sheeler's *Americana* and O'Keeffe's *Lake George Window* (figs. 14, 15) were illustrated side by side. Critic Dorothy Grafly commented upon this comparison: "both here shown in a mood of new-world classicism" due to their "delight in geometrics . . . reduced to photographic purity."[109]

Another artist often associated with the "new spirit of classicism" and the "new objectivity" was the future Public Works of Art project director Edward Bruce. A pupil of Hirsch, friend of Driggs and Leo Stein, Bruce was known since 1922 for the architectonic clarity, simplicity, and severity of his landscapes, which critics related to Oriental art, Cubism, and the Italian primitives. He had a one man show at the Milch Galleries, New York, of his urban and industrial paintings. He received accolades for demonstrating the "accuracy and precision . . . of an architect," exemplified by *Industry* (plate 70) and other works on view.[110]

Bruce's work was occasionally compared to that of O'Keeffe, who had an important retrospective at An American Place in January 1933. In his review of the show, McBride emphasized her paintings of rural vernacular architecture (plate 124), noted for "the exquisite precision with which these barns are placed upon canvas . . . being intellectually arrived at. . . . the mechanics . . . so successfully concealed."[111]

One of O'Keeffe's barn pictures was included, along with works by Sheeler, Spencer, and Davis, in a group exhibition at the Downtown Gallery in March 1935. The intention of the show was to represent the true, cosmopolitan American Scene, based on "a broad universal language rather than an expression of limited provincialism" exemplified by the midwestern Benton-Wood-Curry School, which eschewed foreign influences.[112] This challenging exhibition coincided with the Whitney Museum's controversial, pioneering survey of abstract painting in America, which demonstrated the variety and vitality of this idiom, which had roots in a number of international styles. The Precisionists were well represented in the show, with works of 1918–32 by Ault, Billings, Demuth, Dickinson, Hirsch, Horter, O'Keeffe, Schamberg, Sheeler, and Spencer. Also represented were Stella and particularly Davis, who wrote the introduction. Reviewers drew a distinction between Davis as a true practitioner of Cubist abstraction and such Precisionists as Dickinson, "who used cubism to clarify their ideas in art—an experimentation which added plastic significance to their later representational work."[113]

Another artist featured was painter, printmaker, commercial illustrator, and collector Earl Horter, who also lent two works by Sheeler, including the Precisionist yet mysterious *Stairway to the Studio*, 1924 (Philadelphia Museum of Art). Horter's fine modern-art collection, which also comprised works by Picasso, Braque, Matisse, Duchamp, Gris, and Brancusi, was an important resource for himself and other Philadelphia artists. Horter appreciated Sheeler as "one of the most selective artists in painting" and believed his *Stairway to the Studio* to be "perfectly designed."[114] By 1931, Horter had created a series of works, based on his preferred architectural subject matter, that are skillful, original adaptations of Sheeler's Precisionist aesthetic (plate 32).

At the time of his joint exhibition with Charles Burchfield at the Detroit Society of Arts and Crafts in 1935, Sheeler was called the "precisionist par excellence."[115] As such, he set the standard for a younger generation of artists, including the art historian Wade White (plate 36) and Edmund Lewandowski.[116] The latter has extended the Precisionist aesthetic to the present time and to the Midwest. Raised in the industrial city of Milwaukee, Lewandowski also appreciated the rural aspects of his environment and painted a series known as Farmscapes of the Midwest (plate 126). In these paintings, he focused on the linear, vernacular design of barns rather than on nature. He later observed that there "seemed to be a relationship of architectonic contents between the cityscapes, factories, and the farmscape forms."[117]

By 1936, Lewandowski had achieved acclaim as a WPA painter. In November of that year, he joined the Downtown Gallery. Halpert and other critics repeatedly compared his work to Sheeler's, with which he had only recently become acquainted. Since then, Lewandowski has considered Sheeler to be his primary mentor and influence. Sheeler also recommended the younger artist for many commissions for paintings of American industry. His noncommissioned works of 1939, *Insulators* and *Industrial Composition* (plates 81, 82), both based upon the vast, diversified Allis-Chalmers complex near Milwaukee, reflect his lifelong fascination with technological power and the precision of functional design, which he distills into highly ordered, timeless, depopulated compositions, stripped of nonessentials.

Lewandowski's Sheeleresque combination of precise realism and strong, underlying abstract design was also evident in the work of another artist emerging at this time, Ralston Crawford. He too was familiar with the industrialized environment, having grown up amid shipyards, docks, and grain elevators in Ontario and Buffalo. He then attended the Pennsylvania Academy of Fine Arts and was introduced to Cézanne, Cubism, and modern art through the Barnes Foundation and several private collections, including that of Horter, where he was also exposed to Sheeler's work. Based in New York in 1934, he began to paint industrial, urban, maritime, and rural subjects in a hard-edged, simplified, unmodulated style that situated his work within the Precisionist movement (plate 75). Moving to Exton, Pennsylvania, in 1935, Crawford painted the barns of that region (plate 132), one of which was characterized in a review of 1936 as possessing "the satisfying cleanliness of Sheeler, but without his photographic qualities."[118] By the time of his first New York one-man show in 1939, Crawford was recognized for the "precision of line," "almost classical severity," and "haunting nostalgia" of his distilled, dehumanized industrial subjects, such as the featured *Buffalo Grain Elevators* (plate 77).[119] Also included was *Sanford Tanks No. 2* (plate 80), related to his photographic studies of Florida gas tanks. Attracted to the sculptural contrasts of cylindrical and rectangular forms offered by these sites, Crawford developed an evocative vocabulary of increasingly bolder planarity, simplification, and abstraction that would distinguish his work from that of Sheeler and other Precisionists.

While Sheeler set the standard for some of the younger, emerging Precisionists, others, such as Virginia Berresford, were also compared to Demuth and O'Keeffe. While studying privately with Ozenfant in Paris from 1925 to 1930, Berresford received extensive training in the tenets of Purism, which later guided her to an appreciation of factories in New Bedford, Massachusetts (plate 76): "They were good vehicles for simplicity, for a purely abstract thinking about color, form, design, and composition."[120] Back in New York, she continued her studies with Ozenfant and became familiar with the work of Sheeler, Demuth, Lozowick, and especially O'Keeffe. In 1936, James W. Lane claimed that Berresford's "clear, simple designs" of varied subjects in her solo show ensured "her place among 'The Immaculates.' "[121]

That year Lane identified Demuth as a "true 'Immaculate' in precision, refinement of line, and selective ability," who, furthermore, "had the inner feeling, a splendid detachment, that fused his art into an emotionally moving whole and kept it from being—what the art of some of the other 'Immaculates' has become—soul less."[122] In 1937, Demuth was the subject of a highly acclaimed retrospective at the Whitney Museum. Critics perceived the "immaculate precision," "intellectual serenity," and disciplined "quality of architectural design that carries over from the actual architectural subjects into many of the flower studies [and still lifes]"[123] (plates 96, 97, 105). Hailed as a master architect of painting, "among the first to see beauty in the visible symbols of modern life," Demuth was distinguished from contemporary artists of the American Scene by his refusal to "analyze their social significance."[124]

Although Demuth was not labeled as a Precisionist in the press coverage of this show, the term appeared in a review of the 1937 Whitney Museum Annual referring to Francis Criss as "another precisionist, . . . [who] thrusts a quirk" into his painting[125] (plates 33, 37). The term "precisionist" appears again in 1938 in Alfred Barr's introduction to an exhibition catalogue surveying three centuries of American art: "The extraordinary technical refinement of Demuth, Dickinson, Sheeler, and Blume have caused some critics to speak of an 'immaculate' or 'precisionist' school of American painting."[126]

That year also saw the publication of Constance Rourke's significant study on Sheeler. Although she did not place Sheeler in the context of a Precisionist or Immaculate School, Rourke articulated many of the aspects of his work that have come to be associated with Precisionism. Her central thesis revolved around the avant-garde redefinition of "classic" as comprising the simple, unornamented, absolute forms of American folk art and vernacular architecture. Thus Sheeler's self-effacing application of the Shaker sense of proportion and simplicity to all his subjects ensured his status as a classic modern master.[127]

As pioneering proponents of folk art, Cahill and Halpert supported Rourke's treatment of Sheeler as an artist continuing early American traditions. Halpert's American Folk Art Gallery and her *American Ancestors* exhibitions (the first of which opened in 1931, after Sheeler's show) established these links with William Harnett, Edward Hicks, and others. Indeed, one of Sheeler's "immaculate" interior scenes was credited with "stand[ing] up very well beside Harnett's masterly *trompe l'oeil*" still life of 1878.[128]

Sheeler was characterized as distinctly American and essentially modern in the press release for his first retrospective at The Museum of Modern Art in 1939. The catalogue introduction was written by Sheeler's longtime friend the poet William Carlos Williams, who praised "the bewildering directness of his vision, without blur" and his "subtler particularization, the abstract . . . left by the artist integral with its native detail."[129] Only the fifth living American artist to be honored with a retrospective at the Modern, Sheeler received much publicity, mostly summarizing his development from Cubist abstraction to his pure, meticulous realism informed by an underlying abstract structure. While Lane praised his "immaculatism" based on "precision, sharpness, the angles of architecture, the clean metallic beauty of engineering," Elizabeth McCausland criticized him for selecting only "what is appropriate to his neat geometrical vision" and ignoring the "tension and struggle of the modern industrial world," where "at any moment in front of these magnificent and immaculate cylinders, police may shoot pickets in the back."[130]

This type of criticism had increased by the time of Sheeler's 1940 exhibition at the Downtown Gallery of his Power series (plates 83, 85), which was commissioned and published by *Fortune* magazine. While McBride praised Sheeler for retaining "the precision of the camera" and eliminating unnecessary photographic detail in order to "present the very spirit . . . of the machine represented," Jewell declared that there "is as much passion in Sheeler's painting as in the machines he paints—and considerably less oil."[131] The pioneering historian of American art Milton Brown regarded the paintings as lifeless, colored photographs: "He emphasizes the precision and pristine clarity of the static forms with the same fragile coldness which Georgia O'Keeffe gives to her flower pieces. . . . He is interested only in the static shell, in its beauty and economy of form without its throbbing internal life."[132] By this time, Milton Brown had already been working on the first comprehensive scholarly study of Precisionism.

THE 1940s TO THE PRESENT

Although Precisionism was entering the annals of history during the later 1940s, the movement was still recognized as a current tendency in exhibition reviews of the early part of the decade. The "precision painting" of Sheeler was recognized as one of "the currents cutting through the general pattern" of the 1940–41 Whitney Annual—encompassing the semiabstractions of Crawford and Criss and the hard-edge, nonobjective paintings of such American Abstract Artist members as Paul Kelpe.[133]

In his introduction to the Carnegie Institute's large survey of American painting in 1940, director Homer St. Gaudens concluded that there were two groups of American Scene painters: "One section with Charles Sheeler constructs its results with steel-like precision. The other . . . presents the essence of our social order by way of homely anecdote."[134] This distinction was also made in the catalogue for an important group show of 1941 at the Cincinnati Art Museum, *A New Realism*. Thirty-eight works by Sheeler, Demuth, Spencer, and Crawford were presented as evidence of their discovery of "forms and abstract qualities in America's industrial landscape that led to another 'New Realism,'" distinct from that of the American Scene painters.[135]

The Precisionists were placed within a broad American context in The Museum of Modern Art's ground-breaking show of 1943, *American Realists and Magic Realists*. Curator Dorothy Miller stated that it emphasized "pictures of *sharp focus and precise representation*, whether the subject has been observed in the outer world—*realism*, or contrived by the imagination—*magic realism*."[136] The show opened with a section devoted to such nineteenth-century precursors as Raphaelle Peale, Harnett, Thomas Eakins, and Hicks. Observing that their "strong interest in minute realism became almost extinct" with the prominence of Henri and the Eight, Miller attributed its resurgence to Sheeler in the 1920s: "By 1925 a fresh approach to realism had been made by Charles Sheeler, who combined the precision of his previous abstract painting and of his camera in a style which has become an archetype for much of the work in this exhibition. . . . Before the end of the 1920s, Demuth, Dickinson, and O'Keeffe had become known as precisionists, but it is Sheeler who stands at the heart of the movement."[137] To emphasize his status as a pioneer, Miller placed Sheeler's work with that of the nineteenth-century painters. This section was followed by the contributions of twenty-six contemporaries. Among them were Blume, Lewandowski, Lozowick, and Miklos Suba, a Hungarian-born painter and architect based in Brooklyn.

The Museum of Modern Art's exhibition received considerable press coverage that raised unanswered questions about the confusing relationship of Precisionism to Realism and Magic Realism. Called the "most objective of the twentieth-century American realists, leader of what is sometimes called the 'Frigidaire' School of U.S. painting," Sheeler was named, along with Lozowick, head of a current that was separate from other forms of realism: "[The] 'mechanists' . . . Charles Sheeler . . . and Louis Lozowick . . . belong not to the tradition of meticulous realism, but to an important modern artistic tendency which introduced the machine as subject matter and certain of its stylistic corollaries into the body of contemporary art. This group has only one trait in common with the others—precision. Precision is for them, however, a fundamental quality of the machine and is used as an expressive means and not as a technical *tour de force*."[138]

This emphasis on Precisionism as an aesthetic based on the machine had already been developed by Brown. Although his ground-breaking article, "Cubist-Realism: An American Style," did not appear until the 1943–45 issue of *Marsyas*, he wrote it before the war as a chapter of his dissertation on twentieth-century American painting. Dissatisfied with the prevalent terminology for Precisionism, which placed a limited emphasis on its hard-edged style, Brown toyed with the term "mechanist" but settled on "Cubist-Realism" to denote the general development "from the use of simple abstract surfaces to the meticulous rendering of nature."[139] Observing that Cubist-Realism was not a school with a manifesto, Brown nevertheless discerned "a recognizable and influential American style" based on an "attempt . . . to impart to all matter a sense of fundamental mass, clarity, and precision" without ornament or "the peculiarities . . . of light, texture, and atmosphere."[140] As the Cubist-Realist tendency developed, the style shed its earlier relationships to Cubism and Futurism and more closely approached direct, realistic representations of mechanical subjects. Placing Cubist-Realism within the context of Purism, Functionalism, and the impact of Duchamp and Picabia, Brown saw Demuth as the innovator and Sheeler as the leading exponent. He divided the movement into two tendencies, based on mechanical and organic representations: "Among the more mechanically minded, besides Sheeler and Schamberg, were . . . Stella, . . . Lozowick, . . . Ault, . . . Spencer, . . . Hirsch, and . . . Billings. To the organic group belonged . . . O'Keeffe, . . . Driggs, and . . . Bruce with his American version of *Neue Sachlichkeit*. Demuth stands somewhere between, equally interested in the mechanical and the organic."[141]

Brown also discussed the early impact of Futurism on Stella and Lozowick, noting that the lingering sense of dynamism in their work "serves to differentiate [them] from the other Cubist-Realists primarily concerned with static mass."[142] He distinguished the "highly personal flavor" of Dickinson's still lifes, observing that "he did not strip the object of all nonessentials . . . but made them elements of the design."[143] Concluding that Cubist-Realism was not a revolutionary style, Brown summarized its importance in establishing "the machine and the industrial scene as . . . central concepts in American art, and, in its insistence on the clean and unencumbered surface, it helped to influence not only a considerable group of artists, but also American taste as a whole."[144]

Around the time of Brown's pivotal article, the terms "precisionist" and "precisionism" were employed with growing frequency. In 1943, Zoltan Sepeshy, of the Cranbrook Academy of Art, Bloomfield Hills, Michigan, referred to "precisionism," along with surrealism, abstractionism, romanticism, and American Scene painting as "facets of one crystal . . . to be cemented together" to create a new, "genuinely balanced [postwar] art."[145] Crawford was called a precisionist when in 1946 he exhibited his geometric abstract paintings based on the atom bomb tests at Bikini Atoll; according to one critic, this "precisionist's neatly compiled calculations" did not "successfully convey the 'feel' of the utter devastation that followed."[146] When the U.S. State Department's Advancing American Art collection was shown overseas in 1947, Sheeler was promoted as "one of the best known members" of "the group of painters known as precisionists."[147]

The first comprehensive study to employ the term "Precisionism" to characterize the art of

Sheeler and others was written by the German-born scholar Wolfgang Born in 1947. In *Still-Life Painting in America*, Born traced the history of this subject from the Peale family to the Precisionists, emphasizing a continuous "genuine American tradition. . . . of seeing that may be called matter of fact, detached, sober, spare, puritan."[148] According to Born, in the chapter "The Growth of Precisionism," the movement evolved from the independent experiments of Demuth, Dickinson, and Sheeler, who all exhibited at the Daniel Gallery.

Emphasizing the American inclination toward detached, scientific exactitude, Born developed his ideas on Precisionism further in his 1948 book *American Landscape Painting* in a chapter entitled "A Technocratic Landscape." He credited Stieglitz with "paving the way for a distinctly . . . 'objective' style of photography that formed the starting point for. . . . precisionism, an art that was to combine the exactitude of photography with the geometrical interpretation of space introduced by cubism."[149] In this book, Born shifted his emphasis somewhat to the importance of the vernacular in Sheeler's development of an essential Precisionist style out of "an integration of the photographic attitude with the requirements of a cubism that was . . . more influenced by Shaker design than by French art."[150] Later art historians such as Barbara Novak would also link Precisionism to earlier American traditions, especially the luminist landscapes of Fitz Hugh Lane and others—"an art that . . . tended toward the measured and planar . . . smooth-surfaced and anonymous . . . timeless and contained. . . . [a] fusion of the real and ideal."[151]

Around the time Born's first book was published, Halpert began promoting certain Downtown Gallery artists as Precisionists. In November 1947, she publicized Spencer's first show in many years, stating that the 1920s works he exhibited "demonstrate[d] that [he] was always in the avant-garde, a charter member of the so-called 'precisionist' school."[152] In 1949, Halpert characterized Sheeler as a "pioneer American abstractionist, subsequently recognized as founder of the 'precisionist' school . . . and a leader of the magic-realists."[153] In 1950, she held exhibitions of Crawford and Demuth's paintings, stating that the former had developed "from the 'precisionist' movement" and that the latter was "represented in all his moods from the early romantic period to his late precisionist style."[154]

In 1951, the scholar John I. H. Baur rejected the term "Precisionism," reverting to the usage of the "Immaculate" label. Regarding the Immaculates as "the backbone of our second period of abstract art in the 1920's," Baur defined the movement as "the first important bridge between native tradition and the modern vision."[155] Baur believed that Demuth, Dickinson, Sheeler, and O'Keeffe were the main figures in this "group of artists who fashioned the principal compromise between abstract principles and American realism," employing a "smooth, precise technique" in "compositions of sharp-edged, simplified forms painted in large areas of unmodulated color."[156] If Demuth established the style's essential features and mechanical subject in *Paquebot "Paris,"* Sheeler established its range, from the abstract *Church Street El* to the realist *Upper Deck*, "about as far towards realism as the Immaculate style could go without losing its preponderantly abstract character."[157]

Despite Baur's authoritative study, critics persisted in using the term "precisionist," notably in articles written about Spencer at the time of his death, in 1952, and his 1954 memorial exhibition at The Museum of Modern Art: "In esthetic and technique the context of Spencer's art is cubism, but the personal quality, the dignity, the distance, and precision are those of the classic. [He] has been called a precisionist—but there is too much human warmth in this work to call it precisionist."[158] Henry McBride, however, remembered Spencer as one of the "real heroes," along with Demuth and Dickinson, "in the 1920s . . . [of] a group of clear-cut American painters who shortly became known as the Immaculates."[159]

In 1959, Martin Friedman, Acting Director of the Walker Art Center, Minneapolis, wrote to Sheeler about his plans for a definitive show entitled *The Immaculates*.[160] Later that year, Friedman interviewed Sheeler about the origins and collective identity of Precisionism. Asserting that the artists had practically "no association with each other," Sheeler claimed that "a group of painters of their own volition . . . just began to paint in a more exacting way . . . to present the subject in itself without the distraction of the means . . . and that meant a precision . . . [which] is as near as [the label] comes to being justified."[161] When asked who the members of the group were, Sheeler mentioned Demuth, Dickinson (although he "never . . . reached the point of precision that Demuth or myself did"), as well as O'Keeffe and Ault.[162] He hesitated to include the latter two artists because of the element of symbolism in their work.

The first of its kind, Friedman's comprehensive exhibition, retitled *The Precisionist View in American Art*, opened in 1960 with over seventy works from 1915 to 1960 by sixteen painters. In the accompanying catalogue, Friedman emphasized the broad range of the movement, which was defined primarily by the stylistic criteria of selective realism: "an idealized [timeless] state of absolute order. . . . brought to an icily defined and flawless finish" through "simplification of form, unwavering, sharp delineation, and carefully reasoned abstract organization."[163] He also regarded the Precisionists' attraction to urban and industrial themes as a unifying characteristic, a view that somewhat minimized the considerable role of still life and rural subjects. Referring only in passing to the vague origins of the term "Precisionism," Friedman merely listed Born's book on still life in the bibliography. He traced the centers of activity and what he determined to be the range of influences on Precisionism, including Surrealism. Unlike Brown and Baur, Friedman confusingly expanded the Precisionist movement (which he defined as "curiously impersonal") to encompass the subjective, hyper-real, Surrealist-influenced work of O. Louis Guglielmi.[164] The diverse exhibition drew praise and criticism as to the various ways in which artists defied and reinforced the broadly defined premises of Precisionism and whether it "really existed as a style and an idea."[165]

Friedman's definitions and varied roster of Precisionists have served as the basis for most subsequent studies and exhibitions on the subject. Susan Fillin-Yeh curated the next significant group show in 1978, selecting fewer artists and elaborating upon the impact of machine-age aesthetics and vocabulary as a basis for the Precisionist style and concept.[166] The influence of technology was also emphasized by Bernhard Schulz in his comprehensive essay of 1980 for an exhibition of modern American art in Germany. In addition, Schulz discussed the influence of historical traditions (for example, Shaker aesthetics on Sheeler), and thereby briefly resurrected the argument in Born's book on still-life painting.[167] Nevertheless, Born's coherent definition of Precisionism was overlooked by Karen Tsujimoto, the author of the catalogue accompanying the most recent large-scale survey exhibition in 1982, *Images of America: Precisionist Painting and Modern Photography*, which originated at the San Francisco Museum of Modern Art. Referring to the origins of the term "Precisionism" as vague and undocumented, Tsujimoto developed further the broad foundation established by Friedman. For the first time in a group show on this subject, the integral connection between photography and Precisionist painting was emphasized, especially through the inclusion of Sheeler's works in both media. Yet critics commented on the overload of photographs, which constituted over half the works in the show, almost transforming a primarily Eastern phenomenon into a survey of straight photography (that is, nonpainterly, nonpictorialist, but rather sharp-focus, objectivist) on the West Coast.[168]

Reacting to this diffuse interpretation, Rick Stewart in 1983 wrote an important focused redefinition of Precisionism that has served as the foundation for subsequent studies. His article was drawn from his 1981 dissertation, in which he proposed that Precisionism was "a definable style" based not so much on "worship of the machine" but rather "the adaptation of science-oriented methods to visual perception. . . . a fundamental reordering of reality brought about by the rise of an Objectivist aesthetic" in painting and literature.[169] He presented Sheeler as the one true Precisionist who coupled this objectivist sense of form, nurtured by straight photography and Cubism, with the concept of place developed by his friend William Carlos Williams. What Williams and others called "the local" would be universalized as pure forms manifested in the reality of subject matter drawn from the artist's native locale. This notion provides a context for Sheeler's emphasis upon still life during the 1920s (especially after 1923, when he met Williams).

Regarding the tension between local, objective reality and universal, abstract design as a hallmark of Precisionism, Stewart defined earlier works of Sheeler's such as *Church Street El* as too abstract and therefore Cubist-Realist in style. Employing Sheeler's *Upper Deck* as the standard, he made similar distinctions when discussing the only other artists who, in his opinion, created truly Precisionist work: Ault, Crawford, Driggs, Lozowick, O'Keeffe, and Spencer. Thus he characterized Lozowick's city paintings and Driggs's *Queensborough Bridge* (plate 22) as Constructivist, whereas his *Still Life #2* (plate 100) and her *Pittsburgh* (plate 58) are Precisionist. Stewart concluded that the artists associated with Precisionism formed a recognizable "school," with a pseudo-manifesto—the 1931 Objectivist anthology in *Poetry* magazine.

Expanding upon Stewart's discussions of the importance of still life in Precisionist painting, John Baker in 1987 coined yet another term, "Formalist Realism." In his study of American still-life painting from 1923 to 1936, Baker defined Formalist Realism as "an aesthetic . . . very much the opposite of simplifying and editing [which] emerged among major . . . painters, including Sheeler, Dickinson, and Spencer, who were inspired by French modernism and also were interested in creating a realism less schematic than Precisionism."[170] Thus, Sheeler's spare *Still Life and Shadows* (plate 93) epitomizes Precisionism, whereas *Home Sweet Home* is a Formalist-Realist work.

The most recent studies of Precisionism range from an acceptance of its diverse directions to limiting the roster of artists working in this style. William C. Agee has observed that the Precisionists "adapted a hard-edged, crisp linearity, in dispositions ranging from Cubist realism to full-blown realism. . . . as part of the worldwide search for a more stable, classicizing art, a drive born from the chaos of World War I."[171] The German scholar Wieland Schmied contrasts the Precisionists' exaltation of the industrial world with the more distrustful, subjective, figure-oriented New Objectivity *(Neue Sachlichkeit)*.[172]

In a recent dissertation—the first on the movement as a whole in thirty years—Diana Dimodica Mille simultaneously broadened and focused the discourse on Precisionism. She has demonstrated how Precisionist machine-age aesthetics in painting and photography paralleled those of Purist, Bauhaus, and *Neue Sachlichkeit* artists as well as the earlier nineteenth-century craft or vernacular tradition in America. Mille confined her in-depth discussion of Precisionism to the work of Sheeler, Crawford, and Spencer as the only members of the group who carried the abstract/realist nexus of this movement forth from the 1920s into the 1950s.[173]

CONCLUSION

What was Precisionism? Can one coherent definition and roster of artists emerge from the profusion of literature on the subject? Although the definition of Precisionism will most likely continue to generate controversy, it has been possible to determine more thoroughly how critics of the period perceived the phenomenon. These writers frequently chose the terms "precision," "precise," and "immaculate" to characterize the work of artists as diverse as Demuth and Sheeler, the unofficial leaders of the movement by 1927. Employing a formalistic terminology primarily derived from machine-age aesthetics, critics discussed the range of Precisionist works—urban-industrial, still life, and rural, vernacular subjects—in similar, stylistically coherent terms.

Interpreted as a classic reaction against the impermanent formlessness of Impressionism and the Eight, Precisionism proposed a fundamental reordering of experience, a clarifying search for architectonic structure underlying the chaos of reality. Indeed, metaphors of architecture, science, engineering, and mechanization were often employed to characterize the Precisionists' methodical, rational construction of

16. Stefan Hirsch. *New York, Lower Manhattan.* 1921. Oil on canvas, 20 x 34". The Phillips Collection, Washington, D.C.

compositions. A number of these artists, including Schamberg and Suba, studied architecture. Others, like Sheeler, Lozowick, and Spencer, were strongly linked to industry through their backgrounds or work experiences.

The essence of the Precisionist aesthetic was an objectivist synthesis of abstraction and realism, manifested by hard-edged, static, smoothly brushed, simplified forms rendered in unmodulated colors. Transitory superfluities of expressive painterly process, time, atmosphere, and anecdotal details were removed to varying degrees as barriers to the essential integrity of the object and its direct apprehension. This sober, matter-of-fact mode of perception, nurtured by mechanization and vernacular design, was regarded as distinctively American.

Within the formalist framework of Precisionism, there was a considerable range of individual idioms and attitudes, from the diverse, lyrically nuanced, stylized oeuvre of Demuth to Sheeler's impersonal realism. Even the work of the paradigmatic Precisionist Sheeler extends from the Cubist-Realist *Church Street El* to the photorealism of the Power series. Nevertheless, critics of the period perceived common stylistic attributes and goals among the Precisionists as selective realists who variously distilled the essential forms of a highly refined reality.

Critics also perceived the complex blend of influences that led to the formulation of Precisionism. The constructive emphasis on form in the art of such past masters as Giotto and Cézanne was wedded to the present, postwar "call to order" manifested by Cubism, Purism, and the New Objectivity movements. Among the first artists to create a vocabulary appropriate to the new industrialized age, the Precisionists were also among the pioneers of the period's revival of interest in early American and folk art.

Furthermore, the zeitgeist of the 1910s to the early 1940s, the era's aspirations and conflicts, are evoked by the range of attitudes conveyed in the work of the Precisionists. Lewandowski's unabashed celebrations of America's preeminence as a technological power can be contrasted with Hirsch's hauntingly immobile urban-industrial vistas (fig. 16). Even Sheeler's views of the city and industry, usually seen as optimistic confirmations, have been recently interpreted as revealing the anxieties of individual and artistic identity in an increasingly mechanized, dehumanized, and standardized era.

The end of Precisionism can be linked to the devastations of World War II, which effectively destroyed the machine-age beliefs in industry as a beneficent force. Largely forgotten after the triumphant rise of Abstract Expressionism were the contributions of America's major generation of modernists, active since the 1913 Armory Show. Steering past the potential pitfalls of Regionalism, the Precisionists forged a distinctive, universal synthesis of popular, local subject matter, selective realism, and solid abstract design. They established a significant legacy for succeeding generations of geometric abstractionists, minimalists, photo-realists, and pop artists. Within the pluralistic panorama of contemporary art, their achievements endure.

NOTES

1. Quoted in "The Iconoclastic Opinions of M. Marcel Duchamps [sic] Concerning Art and America," *Current Opinion*, November 1915, p. 346.
2. Quoted in "French Artists Spur On an American Art," *New York Tribune*, October 24, 1915, part IV, p. 2.
3. Autobiographical manuscript, Charles Sheeler Papers, Archives of American Art, Smithsonian Institution, Washington, D.C. (hereafter referred to as AAA), microfilm roll NSH1, frame 78.
4. Quoted in Constance Rourke, *Charles Sheeler: Artist in the American Tradition* (New York: Harcourt, Brace, and Company, 1938), p. 48. Demuth called it "the great picture of our time"; quoted in John Tancock, "The Influence of Marcel Duchamp," in *Marcel Duchamp*, Anne d'Harnoncourt and Kynaston McShine, eds., exh. cat. (New York: The Museum of Modern Art, 1973), p. 163.
5. Quoted in *The Definitively Unfinished Marcel Duchamp*, Thierry Duve, ed. (Cambridge, Massachusetts: The MIT Press, 1991), p. 374. Duchamp's growing interest in precision optics is also pertinent.
6. D'Harnoncourt and McShine, *Marcel Duchamp*, p. 272.
7. Agnes Meyer, "How vs. Why," and statement by Paul Haviland, *291*, March 1915, p. 1, and September–October 1915, p. 1, respectively. William C. Agee, *Morton Livingston Schamberg (1881–1918)*, exh. cat. (New York: Salander O'Reilly Galleries, 1982).
8. *291*, September–October 1915, p. 1.
9. Quoted in Agee, *Schamberg*, p. 12.
10. William C. Agee, "Morton Livingston Schamberg: Notes on the Sources of the Machine Images," in *New York Dada*, Rudolf E. Kuenzli, ed. (New York: Willis Locker and Owens, 1986), pp. 72–73.
11. Quoted in Patrick L. Stewart, "The European Art Invasion: American Art and the Arensberg Circle, 1914–1918," *Arts*, vol. 51, May 1977, p. 110.
12. Quoted in Ruth Cloudman, *Preston Dickinson 1889–1930*, exh. cat. (Lincoln, Nebraska: Sheldon Memorial Art Gallery, 1979), p. 22 and illustrated pp. 71, 75, 79.

13. Review, *The New York Times*, February 18, 1917, p. 14, and Forbes Watson, "At the Art Galleries," *New York Evening Post Magazine*, February 17, 1917, p. 11.
14. See Karen Davies, "Charles Sheeler in Doylestown and the Image of Rural Architecture," *Arts*, vol. 59, March 1985, pp. 135–39, and Henry M. Sayre, "American Vernacular: Objectivism, Precisionism, and the Aesthetics of the Machine," *Twentieth-Century Literature*, vol. 35, Fall 1989, pp. 331–35.
15. Betsy Fahlman, *Pennsylvania Modern: Charles Demuth of Lancaster*, exh. cat. (Philadelphia: Philadelphia Museum of Art, 1983), p. 11.
16. See Barbara Haskell, *Charles Demuth*, exh. cat. (New York: Harry N. Abrams, Inc., 1988), pp. 121–41.
17. Albert Gleizes, "Art European-Art American," *Annual Exhibition of Modern Art Arranged by a Group of European and American Artists in New York* (New York: Bourgeois Galleries, 1919), unpaginated.
18. Henry McBride, "News and Comment in the World of Art," *The New York Sun*, May 25, 1919, p. 12.
19. "La formation de l'optique moderne," reprinted in Amédée Ozenfant and Charles-Édouard Jeanneret, *La Peinture moderne* (Paris: Les Editions G. Crès & Cie, 1925), p. 65 (with photographs of American industrial buildings and skyscrapers; Lozowick's *Cleveland* [plate 15] is illustrated).
20. Bernard De Fayet, "Painting, Past and Present," *Broom*, vol. 3, September 1922, p. 154.
21. Lewis Mumford, "The City," *Civilization in the United States* (New York: Harcourt, Brace, and Co., 1922), p. 12.
22. Louis Lozowick, *Modern Russian Art* (New York: Museum of Modern Art/Société Anonyme, 1925), p. 35.
23. Quoted in James Johnson Sweeney, "Léger and the Cult of the Close-Up," *The Arts*, vol. 27, May 1931, p. 564.
24. Henry McBride, "Salons of America Now Includes Art Specimens," *The New York Herald*, May 27, 1923, p. 7.
25. Lewis Mumford, *Sticks and Stones* (New York: Boni and Liveright, 1924), pp. 179, 219.
26. See Rick Stewart, "Regionalism and the Dial," *The Visionary Company*, vol. 1, summer 1981, p. 110, and Matthew Baigell, "American Art and National Identity: The 1920s," *Arts*, vol. 61, February 1987, pp. 48–55.
27. Holger Cahill, quoted in Doreen Bolger, "Hamilton Easter Field and His Contribution to American Modernism," *The American Art Journal*, vol. 20, 1988, pp. 79–107.
28. Helen Appleton Read, "Introducing the Cigar Store Indian into Art," *The Brooklyn Daily Eagle*, February 17, 1924, p. 2B.
29. Murdock Pemberton, "The Art Galleries," *The New Yorker*, April 9, 1927, p. 114. For a list of reviews of the gallery's shows, see Julie Mellby, "A Record of Charles Daniel and the Daniel Gallery," M.A. thesis, Hunter College of the City University of New York, 1993.
30. Helen Appleton Read, "News and Views on Current Art," *The Brooklyn Daily Eagle*, December 3, 1922, p. 2E.
31. "The World of Art," *The New York Times Book Review and Magazine*, December 19, 1920, p. 20, and Hamilton Easter Field, "Comment on the Arts," *The Arts*, vol. 1, January 1921, p. 31.
32. "Paintings and Drawings by Sheeler," *American Art News*, vol. 20, April 1, 1922, p. 6, and Thomas Craven, "Charles Sheeler," *Shadowland*, vol. 8, March 1923, p. 71.
33. Helen Appleton Read, "New York as Art," *The Brooklyn Daily Eagle*, May 15, 1932, p. E6.
34. See Emily Kies Bardack, "The City and the Machine: Urban and Industrial Illustration in America, 1880–1900," Ph.D. diss., Columbia University, 1971, and Marianne Doezema, "The Clean Machine: Technology in America Magazine Illustration," *Journal of American Culture*, vol. 11, Winter 1988, pp. 73–92.
35. "New York City Offers Artists Rich Material," *The World*, May 4, 1924, p. 8M.
36. Ibid.
37. Forbes Watson, "American Note in Demuth's Art," *The World*, December 2, 1923, p. 8.
38. Forbes Watson, "Dickinson at Daniel's," *The World*, April 27, 1924, p. 9M; Henry McBride, "Notes and Activities," *The New York Sun*, April 26, 1924, p. 6; and Thomas Craven, "Preston Dickinson," *Shadowland*, vol. 6, November 1921, pp. 11, 68.
39. "Art," *The New York Times*, May 4, 1924, p. 10. See Henry McBride, "Art News and Reviews," *The New York Herald*, November 4, 1923, for the word "immaculate."
40. See Merrill Schleier, *The Skyscraper in American Art, 1890–1931* (Ann Arbor: UMI Research Press, 1986), p. 73, and Doezema, "The Clean Machine."
41. "A Group of Moderns," *New York Times*, February 17, 1924, p. 11, and Henry McBride, " 'Moderns' and Others at the Daniel Galleries," *The Sun*, October 25, 1924, p. 3.
42. Paul Rosenfeld, *Port of New York: Essays on Fourteen American Moderns* (1924), quoted in Barbara Buhler Lynes, *O'Keeffe, Stieglitz, and the Critics, 1916–1929* (Chicago: University of Chicago Press, 1991), p. 206.
43. Helen A. Read, quoted in Lynes, p. 202.
44. Quoted in Forbes Watson, "Charles Sheeler," *The Arts*, vol. 3, May 1923, p. 341.
45. Quoted in Lynes, p. 215.
46. Henry McBride, "Art News and Reviews," *The New York Herald*, March 9, 1924, p. 13, and Forbes Watson, "Sheeler Arranges an Abstract Group," *The World*, March 9, 1924. See also Sheeler's appreciation of "the intellectual and precise art" of the Greeks in his review of the Club's Greek art exhibition in *The Arts*, vol. 7, March 1925, p. 153.
47. Forbes Watson, "Selected Works by Sheeler," *The World*, March 16, 1924, p. 8M.
48. Forbes Watson, "Charles Sheeler," *The Arts*, vol. 3, May 1923, p. 341.
49. Helen Appleton Read, "News and Views on Current Art," *Brooklyn Daily Eagle*, January 31, 1926, p. E9.
50. Margaret Breuning, "About Artists and Their Work," *New York Evening Post*, April 11, 1925, section 5, p. 11.
51. Henry McBride, "Joseph Stella's Startling Art," *The Sun*, April 11, 1925, p. 9. For more, see Wendy Jeffers et al., *Niles Spencer* (New York: Whitney Museum of American Art at Equitable Center, 1990).
52. Duncan Phillips, *A Collection in the Making* (New York: E. Weyhe, 1926), p. 11.
53. Ibid, p. 65.
54. Robert Allerton Parker, "The Classical Vision of Charles Sheeler," *International Studio*, vol. 84, May 1926, p. 72. *MacDougal Alley* (plate 12) is illustrated.
55. Ibid, p. 69.
56. Ibid, pp. 70–71.
57. "Charles Sheeler—New Art Circle," *The Art News*, vol. 24, January 23, 1926, p. 7.
58. Louis Rich, "Souls of Our Cities," *The New York Times Magazine*, February 17, 1924, p. 3, and "Newark Museum Art Exhibit Shows American Tendencies of Present Day," *Newark Sunday Call*, April 13, 1924.
59. Lozowick translation of German article by Dietrich, "Louis

Lozowick," *Farbe und Form,* vol. 1, 1923, pp. 4–5, Louis Lozowick Papers, AAA, Roll 1333, frame 10.

60. Robert Wolf, "Louis Lozowick," *The Nation,* vol. 122, February 17, 1926, p. 186. See also Virginia Marquardt, "Louis Lozowick: From 'Machine Ornaments' to Applied Design, 1923–1930," *Journal of Decorative and Propaganda Arts,* vol. 8, Spring 1988, pp. 40–57.

61. "Dudensing Shows Stella's New Work," *Art News,* vol. 24, April 17, 1926, pp. 1, 7. See also Irma B. Jaffe, *Joseph Stella* (New York: Fordham University Press, 1988), pp. 62–63.

62. Helen A. Read, "American Artists at Daniel Galleries," *The Brooklyn Daily Eagle,* April 18, 1926, p. 6E, and Elizabeth L. Cary, "Old and Young Art in the New York Galleries," *The New York Times,* October 31, 1926, section 8, p.11.

63. "Katherine Schmidt, Daniel Gallery," *The Art News,* vol. 25, January 29, 1927, p. 9.

64. "Karl Knaths, Daniel Gallery," *The Art News,* vol. 28, March 1, 1930, p. 12.

65. Duncan Phillips, letter to Charles Daniel, April 20, 1928, Phillips Collection Papers, Phillips Collection Archives, Washington, D.C., microfilmed by AAA, roll 1935, frame 602.

66. Quoted in Lynes, p. 259.

67. Katherine Kuh, *The Artist's Voice* (New York: Harper and Row, 1962), p. 191 (interview). See also Anna C. Chave, " 'Who Will Paint New York?' 'The World's New Art Center' and the Skyscraper Paintings of Georgia O'Keeffe," *American Art,* vol. 5, Winter–Spring 1991, pp. 87–107.

68. Henry McBride, "Work of Eight Painters Shown," *The New York Sun,* April 9, 1927, p. 16.

69. Louis Kalonyme, "Whitney Studio Club Members Exhibit Their Work," *The New York Times,* February 27, 1927, section 7, p. 11.

70. Peter Blume interviewed by Robert Brown, August 16, 1983, transcript, p. 26, AAA, and Driggs interview, October 30, 1985, p. 25, AAA.

71. Alfred Barr, "Tendencies in Modern American Painting" (summary of lecture), *The Bowdoin Orient,* May 11, 1927, pp. 3–4.

72. "May Flowers, Downtown Gallery," *The Art News,* vol. 26, May 5, 1928, p. 12.

73. Quoted in George Ault Papers, AAA, roll D247, frame 17. See also Susan Lubowsky, *George Ault* (New York: The Whitney Museum of American Art, 1988), p. 22: "In this picture, I have . . . demonstrated . . . those essential things that go to make a pictorial composition: the scene that excited my esthetic emotion reduced to the simple forms of which it was composed, leaving out all unessential detail."

74. "George Ault," *The Art News,* vol. 27, December 1, 1928, p. 7, and Margaret Breuning, "George Ault," *The New York Evening Post,* November 24, 1928, p. 10M.

75. "Immaculate School Seen at Daniel's," *The Art News,* vol. 27, November 3, 1928, p. 9.

76. Edward Alden Jewell, "Galleries Offer a Rich Display," *The New York Times,* October 14, 1928, section 10, p. 13.

77. Charles Sheeler, autobiographical manuscript, c. 1938, Sheeler Papers, microfilm roll NSH1, frame 122.

78. Elsie Driggs interviewed by Francine Tyler, transcript pp. 2, 22, 75, and passim, AAA.

79 "American Art Has Numerous Styles" (summary of lecture), *Wellesley College News,* vol. 37, May 9, 1929, pp. 1–2. See also announcement for "A Course of Five Lectures on Modern Art," April and May 1929, reprinted in Irving Sandler et al., *Defining Modern Art* (New York: Abrams, 1986), p. 68.

80. "Group Exhibition: Daniel Gallery," *The Art News,* vol. 27, March 16, 1929, p. 11.

81. Helen Appleton Read, "Daniel Gallery Opens with American Group," *The Brooklyn Daily Eagle,* November 3, 1929, p. E7.

82. Henry McBride, "Born American and Others," *The New York Sun,* October 26, 1929, p. 10.

83. Charles Sheeler, autobiographical manuscript, microfilm roll NSH1, frames 105, 113.

84. Charles Sheeler, "A Brief Note on the Exhibition," *Charles Sheeler,* exh. cat. (New York: The Museum of Modern Art, 1939), p. 11.

85. Sheeler autobiographical manuscript, microfilm roll NSH1, frame 107.

86. Sheeler, "A Brief Note," p. 10.

87. Samuel M. Kootz, *Modern American Painters* (New York: Brewer and Warren, Inc., 1930), p. 35.

88. Ibid, p. 51,

89. Ibid, pp. 18, 32.

90. Ibid, p. 27.

91. "Peter Blume, Daniel Gallery," *The Art News,* vol. 28, February 8, 1930, p. 15.

92. Charles P. Daniel, letter to Ferdinand Howald, July 18, 1931, Ferdinand Howald Papers, AAA, roll 955, frame 114.

93. Donald G. Parker and Warren Herendeen, "An Interview with Peter Blume, Part II," *The Visionary Company,* vol. 1, Summer 1981, p. 64.

94. Ibid, p. 46.

95. Ralph Flint, "Around the Galleries," *Creative Art,* vol. 6, March 1930, sup. 67; K.G.S., "Exhibition by Rosella Hartman," *The New York Times,* December 4, 1931, p. 26; and Virginia Nirdlinger, "In the New York Galleries," *Parnassus,* vol. 4, January 1932, p. 41.

96. Reviews of "Seven Masters of Watercolor," *The New York Herald Tribune* and *New York Times,* March 22, 1931, Downtown Gallery Papers, AAA, ND/52(B), frames 563–66.

97. Undated clipping from *The Tribune,* Valentine Dudensing Papers, AAA, roll 3830, frame [125], and Lloyd Goodrich, "In the Galleries," *The Arts,* vol. 16, February 1930, p. 432.

98. Diane Kelder, ed., *Stuart Davis* (New York, 1971), pp. 33–38, 42, 51.

99. Edith Halpert, letter to Preston Harrison, April 4, 1931, Downtown Gallery Papers, AAA, Box 136. Partly quoted in Diane Tepfer, "Edith Gregor Halpert and the Downtown Gallery downtown: 1926–1940; a study in American art patronage," Ph.D. diss., University of Michigan, 1989, p. 81. On Davis, see Lowery Stokes Sims et al., *Stuart Davis American Painter,* exh. cat. (New York: The Metropolitan Museum of Art, 1991).

100. Alfred H. Barr Jr., *German Painting and Sculpture,* exh. cat. (New York: The Museum of Modern Art, 1931), pp. 12–13.

101. Alfred H. Barr Jr., "Postwar Painting in Europe," *Parnassus,* vol. 3, May 1931, p. 21.

102. "Arnold Wiltz: An Important German-American New Objectivist," *The Art News,* vol. 36, November 6, 1937, p. 16, "Arnold Wiltz–Painter," *Index of Twentieth-Century Artists,* vol. 4, January 1937, p. 677, and Tom Wolf, *Woodstock's Art Heritage* (Woodstock: Overlook Press, 1987), pp. 144–45.

103. Quoted in press release, November 11, 1931, Downtown Gallery Papers, AAA, Box 132.

104. Rourke, *Charles Sheeler,* pp. 183–84. See also Karen Lucic, "Charles Sheeler and Henry Ford: A Craft Heritage for the Machine Age," *Bulletin of the Detroit Institute of Arts,* vol. 65, no. 1, 1989, p. 44.

105. See Lucic, "Charles Sheeler and Henry Ford," p. 39, and Ernest

Brace, "Charles Sheeler," *Creative Art,* vol. 11, October 1932, p. 97.
106. Holger Cahill, *American Painting and Sculpture 1862–1932,* exh. cat. (New York: The Museum of Modern Art, 1932), p. 19.
107. Ibid.
108. Ibid. See also Holger Cahill, "American Art Today," in Fred J. Ringel, ed., *America as Americans See It* (New York: The Literary Guild, 1932), p. 258; and Holger Cahill and Alfred H. Barr Jr., *Art in America: A Complete Survey* (New York: Reynal & Hitchcock, 1935), pp. 95–99. In the 1932 book, Cahill emphasizes the Precisionists' range "from the practitioners of a selective realism . . . to abstractionists and inventors," p. 258. Cahill added Ault, Billings, Criss, Driggs, Goeller, and Wiltz to the list of Precisionists for their clarity of design and excellent feeling for architectonic arrangement.
109. Dorothy Grafly, "The Whitney Museum's Biennial," *American Magazine of Art,* vol. 26, January 1933, pp. 8, 10.
110. Margaretta Salinger, "On View at the New York Galleries," *Parnassus,* vol. 4, November 1932, p. 10, and Bruce Papers, AAA, roll D91, passim.
111. Henry McBride, "Georgia O'Keeffe's Exhibition," *The New York Sun,* January 14, 1933, p. 10. O'Keeffe recalled her barn paintings many years later when she was asked to comment upon the label "Precisionist," "I'm not a joiner and I'm not a precisionist or anything else. It's curious that the show [of 1960] didn't stress what really might have been called precise in my work—the Canadian barns." Quoted in Katherine Kuh, *The Artist's Voice* (New York, 1962), p. 202.
112. "Mrs. Halpert's 'American Scene' Differs From Mid-Western School," *The Art Digest,* vol. 9, March 15, 1935, p. 10.
113. Helen Appleton Read, "The Whitney Museum Presents the Case for Abstract Art," *The Brooklyn Daily Eagle,* February 24, 1935, p. C5.
114. Earl Horter, "Contemporary Painting of the Modern School," exhibition brochure, Smith College Museum of Art, 1930, unpaginated. For more on Horter, see his papers, AAA, roll 4548.
115. "Fogg Museum Acquires Unusual Sheeler," *The Art Digest,* vol. 9, January 15, 1935, p. 6.
116. See Janet Marqusee, *Wade White, 1930's Precisionist* (New York: Janet Marqusee Fine Arts, Ltd., 1989).
117. Letters to the author, July 16 and September 13, 1993.
118. R.F., "New Exhibitions of the Week—A Philadelphia Gallery Comes to New York," *The Art News,* vol. 25, December 5, 1936, p. 15.
119. See Weldon Bailey, Introduction, *Ralston Crawford Paintings* (New York: Boyer Galleries, 1939), unpaginated; "New York," *The Studio,* vol. 117, May 1939, p. 229; and "Crawford's Abstractions," *The Art Digest,* vol. 13, March 1, 1939, p. 23. See also Barbara Haskell, *Ralston Crawford,* exh. cat. (New York: Whitney Museum of American Art, 1985).
120. Telephone interview with the artist, July 1, 1993. See also Virginia Berresford, *Virginia's Journal* (Martha's Vineyard: Glen Publishing Company, 1989), pp. 18–20, 35.
121. James W. Lane, "Current Exhibitions," *Parnassus,* vol. 8, March 1936, p. 27.
122. James W. Lane, *Masters of American Art* (Boston: Chapman & Grimes, 1936), p. 92.
123. Various clippings, December 1937, Whitney Museum of American Art Papers, AAA, N593, frames 528–33.
124. Martha Davidson, "Demuth, Architect of Painting," *The Art News,* vol. 36, December 18, 1937, p. 8.
125. Margaret Breuning, "Art Comment," *New York Post,* undated clipping, Downtown Gallery Papers, AAA, ND55, frame 100.
126. Alfred H. Barr Jr., *Trois Siècles d'art aux Etats-Unis,* exh. cat. (New York: The Museum of Modern Art, 1938), p. 29.

127. See Joan Shelley Rubin, "A Convergence of Vision: Constance Rourke, Charles Sheeler, and American Art," *American Art Quarterly,* vol. 42, June 1990, pp. 191–222.
128. J.L., "A Gallery's Review of the Season," *The Art News,* vol. 38, April 20, 1940, p. 13.
129. William Carlos Williams, Introduction, *Charles Sheeler,* exh. cat. (New York: The Museum of Modern Art, 1939), pp. 6, 8.
130. James W. Lane, "Of Sheeler's Immaculatism," *The Art News,* vol. 38, October 7, 1939, p. 10, and Elizabeth McCausland, "Charles Sheeler Show at Modern Museum," *Springfield Republican,* October 8, 1939, passim, Public Information Scrapbook, The Museum of Modern Art Archives, New York.
131. Henry McBride, "Groups and Individuals," *The New York Sun,* December 7, 1940, Downtown Gallery Papers, AAA, ND41, frame 183, and Edward Alden Jewell, "In the Realm of Art: A Flood of Gallery Exhibitions," *The New York Times,* December 8, 1940, section 10, part 2, p. 13. On this series, see Carol Troyen et al., *Charles Sheeler* (Boston: Museum of Fine Arts, 1987), pp. 164–74.
132. Milton Brown, "Exhibitions-New York," *Parnassus,* vol. 13, January 1941, p. 46.
133. "Whitney Museum Opens Its Best and Largest Painting Annual," *The Art Digest,* vol. 15, December 1, 1940, p. 6.
134. Homer St. Gaudens, Introduction, *Survey of American Painting,* exh. cat. (Pittsburgh: Carnegie Institute, 1940), unpaginated.
135. Elizabeth Sacartoff, Introduction, *A New Realism,* exh. cat. (Cincinnati: Cincinnati Art Museum, 1941), p. 3.
136. Dorothy Miller, Foreword and Acknowledgments, *American Realists and Magic Realists,* exh. cat. (New York: The Museum of Modern Art, 1943), p. 5.
137. Ibid, p. 6.
138. Doris Brian, "Is the Sharp Focus Clear?," *Art News,* vol. 42, March 1–14, 1943, pp. 18–20, 26, and Mayer Symason, "Realism as an Escape," *New Masses,* March 9, 1943, Public Information Scrapbook, The Museum of Modern Art Archives, New York.
139. Milton Brown, "Cubist-Realism: An American Style," *Marsyas,* vol. 3, 1943–45, p. 157, and interview with the author, July 12, 1993. The Precisionists were also called the sterilists, according to Brown. Brown's dissertation was published as *American Painting from the Armory Show to the Depression* (Princeton: Princeton University Press, 1955).
140. Brown, "Cubist-Realism," p. 146.
141. Ibid, pp. 151–52.
142. Ibid, p. 152.
143. Ibid, pp. 152, 157.
144. Ibid, p. 158. For Brown's later publications in which he adopted the term "Precisionism," see the Bibliography.
145. "An Art Digest Forum: What Place Art in the Post-War World?" *The Art Digest,* vol. 17, August 1, 1943, pp. 12–13.
146. "Groups and Solos Now on Exhibition," *New York Sun,* December 6, 1946, Downtown Gallery Papers, AAA, ND4, frame 104.
147. Hugo Weisgall, *Advancing American Art* (Prague: U.S. Information Service, 1947), unpaginated.
148. Wolfgang Born, *Still-Life Painting in America* (New York: Oxford University Press, 1947), p. 44. Dickinson's *Hospitality* (plate 91) and Sheeler's *Still Life and Shadows* and *Cactus* (plates 93, 104) are illustrated.
149. Wolfgang Born, *American Landscape Painting* (New Haven: Yale University Press, 1948), p. 206.
150. Ibid, p. 211.
151. Barbara Novak, *American Painting of the Nineteenth Century*

(New York: Praeger, 1969), pp. 272, 274.
152. Press release, November 3, 1947, Downtown Gallery Papers, AAA, ND58, frame 39.
153. Press release, January 17, 1949, Downtown Gallery Papers, AAA, ND58, frame 115. See also " 'Father of Precisionism' " in "Charles Sheeler," exhibition brochure, The Downtown Gallery, 1966, unpaginated.
154. Press releases, Downtown Gallery Papers, AAA, January 23, 1950 (Crawford), ND74, frame 7, and June 26, 1950 (Demuth), ND58, frame 191.
155. John I.H. Baur, *Revolution and Tradition in Modern American Art* (Cambridge, Massachusetts: Harvard University Press, 1951), p. 7.
156. Ibid, pp. 58–59.
157. Ibid, p. 60.
158. Holger Cahill, "Niles Spencer," *Magazine of Art*, vol. 45, November 1952, p. 313.
159. Henry McBride, "An Elegant American Painter," *Art News*, vol. 53, March 1954, p. 21.
160. Martin Friedman, letter to Charles Sheeler, March 12, 1959, Sheeler Papers, AAA, roll 1811, frame 263.
161. Charles Sheeler interviewed by Martin Friedman, June 18, 1959, AAA, pp. 7, 9.
162. Ibid, p. 10.
163. Martin Friedman, *The Precisionist View in American Art*, exh. cat. (Minneapolis: Walker Art Center, 1960), pp. 12–14. The artists represented were Ault, Blume, Crawford, Davis, Demuth, Dickinson, Driggs, O. Louis Guglielmi, Hirsch, Lewandowski, Lozowick, O'Keeffe, Schamberg, Sheeler, Spencer, and Stella.
164. Ibid, p. 51.
165. Hilton Kramer, "The American Precisionists," *Arts Magazine*, March 1961, p. 37.
166. See Susan Fillin-Yeh, *The Precisionist Painters 1916–1949: Interpretations of a Mechanical Age*, exh. cat. (Huntington, New York: Heckshcher Museum, 1978). Ault, Crawford, Criss, Demuth, Dickinson, Driggs, Hirsch, Lozowick, O'Keeffe, Schamberg, Sheeler, Spencer, and Stella were represented.
167. Bernhard Schulz, "Made in America: Technik und Dingwelt im Präzisionismus," *Amerika: Traum und Depression 1920/40*, exh. cat. (Berlin: Neue Gesellschaft für bildende Kunst, 1980), pp. 72–137.
168. See Rick Stewart, "Charles Sheeler, William Carlos Williams, and Precisionism: A Redefinition," *Arts Magazine*, vol. 58, November 1983, pp. 100–114; Hilton Kramer, " 'Images of America': The Precisionists," *The New Criterion*, vol. 1, December 1982, pp. 48–53; and Susan Noyes Platt, "Precisionism: America's Immaculates," *images & issues*, vol. 3, pp. 22–23.
169. Patrick Leonard Stewart, "Charles Sheeler, William Carlos Williams, and the Development of the Precisionist Aesthetic, 1917–1931," Ph.D. diss., University of Delaware, 1981, p. 9.
170. John Baker, *Henry Lee McFee and Formalist Realism in American Still Life, 1923–1936* (Lewisburg, Virginia: Bucknell University Press, 1987), p. 18.
171. William C. Agee, "Modern American Art: The First Half-Century," *Walker Art Center: Paintings and Sculpture from the Collection*, exh. cat. (Minneapolis: Walker Art Center, 1990), pp. 52–53.
172. Wieland Schmied, "Precisionist View and American Scene: The 1920s," *American Art in the Twentieth Century*, exh. cat. (Munich: Prestel Verlag, 1993), p. 49.
173. Diana Dimodica Mills, "Precisionism in Perspective: Form and Philosophy in Twentieth Century Art," Ph.D. diss., City University of New York, 1993, pp. 67–116.

THE IDEA AND THE FACT: Painting, Photography, Film, Precisionists, and the Real World

Ellen Handy

Photography is nature seen from the eyes outward, painting from the eyes inward. Photography records inalterably the single image, while painting records a plurality of images willfully directed by the artist.
CHARLES SHEELER, 1938[1]

Photography . . . finds its raison d'être, *like all media, in a complete uniqueness of means. This is an unqualified objectivity.*
PAUL STRAND, 1917[2]

IS THERE A PRECISIONIST photography? Is the influence of photography on Precisionism equal and opposite to that of Cubism? How do the twists and turns in the story of emerging modernist photography in America during the early years of this century coincide with or differ from those of the Precisionist painters' history? Most important is this question: How did the Precisionist painters use, alter, or reject photographic seeing in their work?

The present exhibition includes photographs by Ralston Crawford, Imogen Cunningham, Paul Outerbridge, Morton Schamberg, Charles Sheeler, Ralph Steiner, Alfred Stieglitz, Paul Strand, and Edward Weston. Each fits into the Precisionist picture differently. Martin Friedman's ground-breaking 1960 exhibition of Precisionism included no photographs, whereas *Images of America*, organized by Karen Tsujimoto in 1982, presented the work of a wide range of photographers, many not previously linked to Precisionism in any way. Since the Precisionists did not constitute a discrete group, inclusion under this rubric depends on individual scholars' subjective decisions. The list of painters to whom photography was (or might have been) important is much longer than this list of photographers, but questions concerning the impact of photography on individual Precisionist painters lie outside the scope of this essay. Three of the Precisionists—Charles Sheeler, Morton Schamberg, and Ralston Crawford—worked in photography as well as painting.

CAMERA-EYE OBJECTIVITY VS. EXPRESSIONIST CORRESPONDENCE

Art, at all times, has been composed of two elements: the ideà and the fact; that is, the subjective and the objective. It began by being essentially subjective and in its evolution it gradually became essentially objective—culminating, so far as relates to plastic representation by man, in Photography.
MARIUS DE ZAYAS, 1913[3]

For the first half of the twentieth century, two very different normative descriptions of the photographic medium's nature competed for primacy. One argued for the machinelike objectivity of an art that exploited the camera's unique and mechanical nature in generating images. The other considered the camera as merely an instrument through which the purely subjective ideas and soul of an artist were projected. The former position (which could incline both toward extreme realism and toward experimental abstraction) is apparent in Sheeler's photographic work, and, in a more extreme form, in Bauhaus photography. The latter approach is most purely embodied in Stieglitz's Symbolist and Expressionist photographs and writings. Between about 1910 and 1940, these two all but irreconcilable positions became the site and matter of a struggle to define the nature and extent of artistic authority within the photographic community. One of the most interesting aspects of the photography most closely associated with Precisionism is that it has alliances to both of these camps.

More than any other individual, Stieglitz shaped the practice of photography as a fine art in America; he was also a major player in the story of modern art in America as artist, writer, curator, dealer, and collector. Stieglitz championed photography as a fine art at the turn of the century through advocacy of the international photographic style he himself practiced, pictorialism. Initially a distinguished practitioner in this

17. Alfred Stieglitz. *Two Towers.* ca. 1911. Photogravure, 12¾ x 10". The Metropolitan Museum of Art, New York. The Alfred Stieglitz Collection, 1949, 49.55.19

painterly, soft-focus mode, Stieglitz was eventually to reject it vehemently for a more direct, less contrived vision. He sought to establish a tradition based on his own photography, but in the wake of his crusade, other visions of photography, some very different from his own, proliferated.

Between about 1910 and the Second World War, the photographic medium became fully integrated into the international modernist program. Its practitioners and theoreticians articulated a whole constellation of aesthetic issues which set the agenda for succeeding generations of photographers. Many of these are issues that were very important to the photographers allied to the Precisionist cause: photography's struggle to establish itself as a fine art, holding its own in relation to (and initially by emulating) painting; abstract composition in photography; photography's identity as a machine art; advertising as appropriate pursuit or as venal disgrace for the art photographer; sharp focus as the preferred mode in art photography; photography as a modernist art, fully autonomous and aware of its own means and properties.

Over time, the delicately soft focused, wintery street scenes in the pictorialist style with which Stieglitz had won renown gave way to sharply sculptural depictions of skyscrapers seen from high above the ground. Instrumental in Stieglitz's artistic rebirth was the influence of two young artists, Paul Strand, Stieglitz's latest photographic discovery, and another discovery, Georgia O'Keeffe, a painter, his future wife, and the collaborative subject of an extended portrait series executed between 1917 and the 1930s. O'Keeffe and Strand were necessary to him in the formulation of his definitive late style of purist photography.

Initially encouraged in photography by Stieglitz, Sheeler was never a pictorialist and always eschewed the emotional aspects of photography. His photography changed much less over the years than Stieglitz's did. He had begun by assuming the medium's autonomy rather than crusading for it. He used his camera for hire, accepting commissions from glossy magazines, advertising agencies, museums, and art galleries. Always sharply focused, Sheeler's photographs explored the world without attempting to present its user's emotions. In 1923, the two men quarreled, ostensibly because of a review Sheeler wrote about Stieglitz's work, and perhaps also because of Sheeler's insistence on retaining a measure of autonomy from Stieglitz's aesthetic edicts, or his continuing affiliation with Juliana Force and the Whitney Studio Club, and his willingness to use photography as a means of financial support.[4]

By the 1920s, Stieglitz's photographic accomplishments and able propagandizing had helped pave the way not only for Sheeler's measured approach but for the caricaturist-critic Marius de Zayas's emphasis on the objectivity of art and photography (quoted above), which took on the ironic tone of Dada antiaesthetics by the 1920s. De Zayas, Duchamp, and their circle admired seemingly soulless or authorless photography, documents, and advertisements. Much of the new photography of the 1920s and thirties, particularly in Europe, was to move further into the realms of objectivity and away from those of expression.

The distance traveled by Stieglitz himself from his early to later phases can best be measured by looking at a work from each. *Two Towers* (fig. 17), which appeared in *Camera Work* in 1913, recalls some of his earliest New York city views. Stair railings and the front yard saplings of a brownstone are coated in snow, echoing the softening of the camera's slightly unfocused lens that was pictorialism's defining attribute.

By 1932, when Stieglitz photographed *Evening, New York from the Shelton* (plate 34), from his apartment window, the scale of ambition of both city and artist had changed. The tough, magisterial view from the Shelton suggests the great number of towers rising throughout the vast city. Distant, blocky skyscrapers are isolated from each other and from the dark shadowed depths of the city. Stieglitz has abandoned the soft patterning of *Two Towers* in favor of a sharply delineated, fully plastic, dynamic portrait of a powerful city. He had reconsidered the camera's objectivity since 1913 and discovered how he might turn it to his own purposes of expression. As bold as any of the photographs by the young Strand that had startled Stieglitz in 1915, this picture makes of the city a far more emotional arena than Sheeler ever portrayed in his urban views of the 1920s. The city was a fertile ground for the experiments of many photographers, and painters, during the 1910s, twenties, and thirties.

SHEELER, STRAND, THE CUBIST CITY, AND THE MACHINE

> *Your New York is the cubist, the futurist city.*
>
> FRANCIS PICABIA, 1913[5]

> *It was Charles Sheeler who proved that cubism exists in nature and that photography can record it.*
>
> MARIUS DE ZAYAS[6]

> *Today all skyscrapers have been whittled to a point. . . . They whistle, they steam, they moor dirigibles, they wave flags, or they merely aspire. . . . They compete—they pictorialize—and are all the same.*
>
> FRANK LLOYD WRIGHT, 1931[7]

By the second decade of the twentieth century, New York City was a phenomenon of modernity unparalleled anywhere in the world. New York *was* a Cubist city, a Futurist city of geometrical spires where the future seemed to begin happening sooner than it did anywhere else. As urban life was achieving new density and artistic experimentation new velocity, quotidian experience was increasingly pervaded by machines, whether in industry, commerce, the domestic environment, communications, leisure and recreation, transportation, or the arts. John Dos Passos's trilogy of novels of New York life in the twenties, *U.S.A.*, employed narrative devices borrowed from documentary film and photography. Passages he identified as "Newsreels" and "Camera Eye" intermittently appear in the narrative, affording textual versions of still photographic and cinematic cameras' renderings of public and personal events. For the novelist, as for painters and for ordinary citizens, both types of cameras were becoming familiar forms of mediation for the almost unassimilable forms and events that urban life afforded.

In 1920, two young artists collaborated in making a very short film about New York City. Both understood the city to be a visual challenge to the camera. They were not filmmakers by training; one was a photographer by vocation and the other (initially) merely by way of a job. The first was Strand, a member of the Stieglitz circle, and the second was Sheeler, who while maintaining relations with Stieglitz also sought to cultivate rival factions in the New York art world. Sheeler would have called himself a photographer in describing his profession, and a painter in describing his identity. In the years to come, Strand, the photographer, was to work regularly as a filmmaker while continuing to *be* a photographer. Sheeler never made another film, and he maintained a somewhat uneasy balance between the photographs that either facilitated or themselves became his art, and the paintings (increasingly resembling photographs) whose art status was unquestioned. Strand and Sheeler's collaboration resulted in the film *Manhatta* (shot in 1920, first publicly screened in 1921), whose rich imagery of the vast, geometric, and dynamic city accords oddly with its intertitles, excerpts from Walt Whitman's *Leaves of Grass*. Whitman's use of human scale in describing the city of the 1850s and sixties

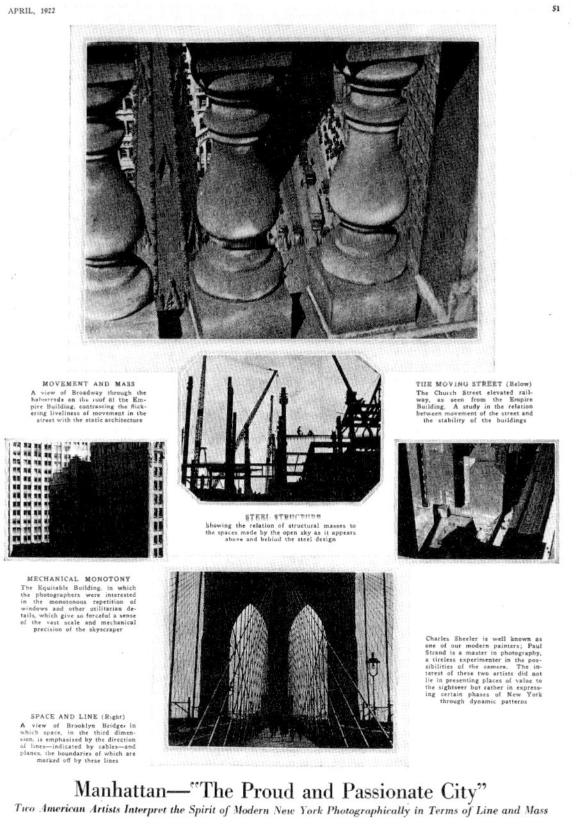
APRIL, 1922 51

MOVEMENT AND MASS
A view of Broadway through the balustrade on the roof of the Empire Building, contrasting the flickering liveliness of movement in the street with the static architecture

THE MOVING STREET (Below)
The Church Street elevated railway, as seen from the Empire Building. A study in the relation between movement of the street and the stability of the buildings

STEEL STRUCTURE
Showing the relation of structural masses to the spaces made by the open sky as it appears above and behind the steel design

MECHANICAL MONOTONY
The Equitable Building, in which the photographers were interested in the monotonous repetition of windows and other utilitarian details, which give so forceful a sense of the vast scale and mechanical precision of the skyscraper

Charles Sheeler is well known as one of our modern painters; Paul Strand is a master in photography, a tireless experimenter in the possibilities of the camera. The interest of these two artists did not lie in presenting places of value to the sightseer but rather in expressing certain phases of New York through dynamic patterns

SPACE AND LINE (Right)
A view of Brooklyn Bridge, in which space, in the third dimension, is emphasized by the direction of lines—indicated by cables—and planes, the boundaries of which are marked off by these lines

Manhattan—"The Proud and Passionate City"

Two American Artists Interpret the Spirit of Modern New York Photographically in Terms of Line and Mass

18. Charles Sheeler. Stills from the film *Manhatta,* published in *Vanity Fair,* vol. 18, April 1922, p. 51. General Research Division, New York Public Library, Astor, Lenox, and Tilden Foundations

Sheeler based his painting *Church Street El* (fig. 5) on the film still at the right of the group, labeled "The Moving Street." Note the author's reference to the Equitable Building as epitomizing the "mechanical precision of the skyscraper."

contrasts with the largely impersonal imagery of the film. The pictured city is animated not by motion within shots or by the actions of individual inhabitants, but by formal devices: abstract patterns, cutting from scene to scene, juxtaposed shapes seen from a skyscraper's point of view. The motion picture camera wielded by the two photographers emphasized the vigor and impressive architectural scale of a lower Manhattan studded with skyscrapers unknown in Whitman's day, when ships' masts and human crowds were the most prominent features of the city. No visual equivalent is offered for the poet's narrative presence—the visual strategies of the film aspire to omniscience rather than to the poem's intimate subjectivity.

As Jan-Christopher Horak has noted, the compositional style of the film is generally more photographic than cinematic, to the point that various specific photographs may be identified as sources for shots in the film.[8] One of these is *Wall Street, New York* (plate 5), an atypically narrative composition by Strand, which combines people with architectural geometry. A frieze of workers is silhouetted against the massive forms of J.P. Morgan's bank at the close of the day. In a press release for the film, Strand wrote that their goal had been:

> *to register through conscious selection and space-filling those elements . . . expressive of the spirit of New York, of its power and beauty and movement . . . [and] was not to be captured through any artifice of diffusion, photographic trickery or superficial picture-making. . . . Restricting themselves definitely to the towering geometry of lower Manhattan and its environs, the photographers have tried to register directly the living forms in front of them. . . . Through these does the spirit manifest itself.*[9]

Though Sheeler gave up filmmaking after this venture, he didn't abandon elevated viewpoints and urban compositions. He continued to paint and draw *Manhatta*-style compositions until the 1950s, and still images from the film appear among his photographic work. Some of these appeared in *Vanity Fair* in April 1922 (fig. 18), credited to both makers, under the heading "Manhattan—'The Proud and Passionate City.' "

By the time he joined forces with Sheeler, Strand had already executed a candid series of clandestine street portraits of working people on the Lower East Side. These were followed by stark abstractions derived from still lifes. Like Sheeler's considered images of the same years, they are reticent in emotional terms—spare and more concerned with abstract visual order than with descriptive rendering of content. Precision, detachment, and a lack of sentimentality were already well established as the defining marks of each man's style. In 1929, Harold Clurman described Strand as seeming "not so much to have detached his material from himself, as . . . to have detached his material from everything else."[10] The remarkable presence and directness of the objects fixed within the frames of each man's photographs was read as an absence of the artist himself—in short, as "detachment."

Sheeler formulated his style in the immediate

wake of the Armory Show of 1913. While supporting himself through commercial photography, he was also painting and photographing at his weekend house in Doylestown, in Bucks County, Pennsylvania, which he shared with Morton Schamberg. Away from the contentious art factions of New York City, Sheeler experimented with photographic composition, both as an end in itself and as a means to subsequent drawn or painted compositions. Schamberg's tantalizingly brief career was also marked by fluid transitions between commercial and fine-art photography, and painting. His photographs won the approval of Stieglitz at the 1918 Wanamaker Salon in Philadelphia, where he awarded Schamberg third prize, with first and fourth prizes going to Sheeler, and second prize to Strand. Schamberg's photographs emphasized the density of the urban scene, as in *Untitled (Cityscape)* (plate 6), which is packed as full of angles and architectural elements as an egg is full of meat. Sheeler's photographs of the mid-teens are simpler and airier. His Doylestown interiors emphasize the sculptural presence of space within the architectural surround or between sparse furnishings (like the central, iconic wood-burning stove that appears in so many of the pictures) in that space. In *Side of White Barn* (plate 107), the building is detached from the immediate context and space is strikingly collapsed to nearly complete flatness in a composition forty-odd years in advance of Greenbergian dictates. Although this barn is pure Americana, the photograph is coolly modern, as definite and architectonic as anything Mondrian was to paint in the next ten years.[11]

At about the same time as Sheeler photographed *Side of White Barn,* Strand was also experimenting in a rural retreat. His *White Fence, Port Kent, New York* (plate 108) compresses spatial planes, eliminating all foreground but the eponymous fence and thus dispensing with any suggestion of distance between the camera and its subject. Striking though this picture's sharp juxtaposition of fence and background are, its spatial construction is less radical (and its detail less lucid) than that of Sheeler's *Barn.* It was to be still life rather than landscape that allowed Strand to use the camera to create compelling and semiabstract compositions, with close framing, unexpected viewpoints, and graphic patterning of light, as in *Still Life: Jug and Fruit, Twin Lakes, Connecticut* (plate 88). The camera looks down at this still life so sharply that the whole appears to tip vertiginously. Brilliant light on the white tabletop washes out surface detail, dematerializing that surface into a floating plane marked only by the shadows of the fruit and jug. Though the table's legs fall outside the plane of focus, blurring from load-bearing support to pattern, the indentations in the oranges' skins remain minutely evident.

What kind of detachment was Strand seeking and expressing in this still life and in his series of photographic abstractions of landmarks? As one of Stieglitz's acolytes, Strand found that his task was to live up to the maestro's expectations and to assert photography's claim to rival painting as a fine-art form in its own right. Thus the series of still lifes Strand made three summers later owes as much to Cézanne's endless variations on the fixity of the object and the fluctuations of perspective and vision as he claimed it does to Picasso. Perhaps it was during work on this series of rigorous experiments that Strand developed what were to become his trademark characteristics: intense resolve and fidelity to the highest standards of technical quality. Strand's abstraction and his characteristic "detachment" here seem synonymous, yet these photographs never entirely renounce representational subject matter. They emphatically are not Cubist in structure, but they do share one of the most salient attributes of that style and of Precisionism: the appearance of abstraction teamed with persistent representation.

Strand's work of circa 1916 is haunted by the difficulty he found in resolving his newly achieved photographic abstraction and his pictorialist past. As he resolved this in favor of sharpness and objectivity of camera vision, his subject matter changed, and the human presence played a smaller role in his work than at any other time. His urban architectural views and machine images of about 1923–24 are immaculate, precise, and somewhat abstract in composition by virtue of close framing of the subjects.

In 1923, Strand turned his view camera on the interior of his shining new Akeley motion picture camera (plate 46), totem of his autonomy in a pictorial realm where Stieglitz's power did not pertain. At once rhapsodic and remote, this photograph honors a beautifully machined artifact, comments on camera art itself, and rejects the idea of human presence in the realm of art. The picture describes a hermetic, magnificently mechanical artistic process; one camera photographed another so that its actual workings are truncated by the closeness of the scrutiny. Strand wrote eloquently about the dangers of the machine in modern society but placed photography in the weighty role of humanity's salvation, an endeavor in which human and machine might meet in partnership. His photograph suggests the desire for, rather than the accomplishment of, that dream.

Strand's machine pictures commemorate the desires of other artists who could approach the machine only indirectly, via metaphor. One poet, William Carlos Williams, declared: "Prose may convey a load of ill defined matters like a ship. But poetry is the machine which drives it, pruned to a perfect economy."[12] Poetry, not just engine but also engineer, thus achieves consciousness by virtue of its "economy." Strand's *Akeley* is sentient in this manner and serves as a stand-in for the poetic engine (camera) with which its portrait was made.

Strand made several related pictures of the Akeley and photographed other machines in a similar fashion—isolated, abstracted, monumentally filling the frame. Sheeler also photographed (and painted) machines during the 1920s, but not in this hermetic fashion. He normally allowed for context, placing the machines in the realm of industry, albeit an idealized industry. Sheeler's subject could better be described as "industry" than as "the machine." He photographed and painted machines as he had skyscrapers, as part of a complex whole embedded in the world, though rather remote from human emotion and experience.

ADVERTISING, INDUSTRY, AND THE REALIGNMENT OF THE PHOTOGRAPHIC AVANT-GARDE

> *Man having created the concept of God the Creator, found himself unsatisfied. . . . Man consummated a new creative act, a new Trinity: God the Machine, Materialistic Empiricism the Son, and Science the Holy Ghost. . . . [There are immense possibilities for the artist] in the creative control of one form of the machine, the camera.*
>
> PAUL STRAND, 1922[13]

> *Industry concerns the greatest numbers—it may be true, as has been said, that our factories are our substitute for religious expression.*
>
> CHARLES SHEELER, 1938[14]

In 1927, Sheeler undertook a photographic commission arranged by the N.W. Ayer advertising agency. The resulting series of photographs of the Ford Motor Company's immense factory in River Rouge, Michigan (plates 54–57), are among his most celebrated works. He left behind the austere vernacular architecture of Bucks County and the alluringly Cubistic readymade compositions of New York skyscrapers for the most advanced factory in the world. Raw ore went in at one end and completed cars rolled off the line at the other, but nothing in Sheeler's photographs illustrates this. Commissioned for general promotional purposes rather than for a specific ad campaign, this job afforded Sheeler the perfect opportunity to pursue some of his own ideas about industrial form.

The most outstanding image from the Ford series is *Criss-Crossed Conveyors* (plate 57). Just off center, a pair of enclosed conveyor belts cross in X formation, their intersection surmounted by the eight tall smokestacks of Ford's powerhouse No. 1. The mightiness of this image has suggested religious meanings to many viewers; *Vanity Fair* reproduced the image in 1928 under the headline "By Their Works Ye Shall Know Them," calling the plant "an American altar of the God-Objective of Mass production."[15] Formal coincidences between the photograph and the views Sheeler was to make of Chartres Cathedral two years later underscore the point. From the enormity and complexity of a factory larger than many small cities, Sheeler selected and defined a view that summarized industry as pure, aspiring magnificence, as aloof as it is superb. Sheeler's photograph is an abstraction of a factory in the same sense that *Manhatta* is an abstraction of a city. This static and monumental place is untenanted by mere humans. Man's role is that of admiring and puny spectator of the industrial world, deprived of the compassionate embrace offered by the machinery to the worker in Lewis Hine's iconic photograph *Steamfitter* (fig. 19), in which harmony assumes the coexistence of man and machine.

19. Lewis Hine. *Steamfitter.* 1921. Gelatin silver print, 16½ x 12". The Metropolitan Museum of Art, New York. Ford Motor Company Collection, Gift of Ford Motor Company and John C. Waddell, 1987.1100.146

After Strand and Sheeler had located machines, rather than individuals or even rush-hour crowds, at the heart of the city in *Manhatta*, Strand had begun a search for photographic origins, a contemplation of his own means of expression that led him to photograph the Akeley camera. But this regression went one step further when he visited the Akeley machine shop to photograph lathes in 1923. He depicted the machines that made the Akeley as fully sculptural objects, more powerful and primal than the delicate, elegant, nearly two dimensional camera (plate 47). Larger (closer) in the frame than the Akeley, the lathes look grinding, powerful, dangerous.

The Cubist city had given way, then, to machines for Strand and to industry on a much larger scale for Sheeler. As the two photographers redefined their interests, machines organized into industrial contexts created mass production, mass markets came into being, and consumerism arose as a social identity and practice. From it and for it, advertising itself became a vast industry, and within advertising appeared the definitive role for photography in the fully industrial society of the mid-twentieth century.

Paul Outerbridge is among the group of photographers renowned for work undertaken for purely commercial purposes. Unlike Sheeler, Outerbridge made his mark in advertising, and only later did his private, noncommercial work become widely known. Although an advertisement, his elegant *Marmon Crankshaft* (plate 48) seems a machine à la Strand and recalls Sheeler's work at Ford. Outerbridge invested the crankshaft with glamorous soft highlights, voluptuously rendering it with attention to its three-dimensionality. His photographs were used in advertisements in the upscale magazines of the day such as *Vanity Fair*, where Sheeler's work appeared both as art and as advertising.

During the 1910s and twenties, modernity in the visual arts was evaluated in part in regard to degree of understanding of abstraction, which was seen as the primary contribution of the Cubist revolution. John Pultz and Catherine Scallen have suggested that pictorialism gave way to a full-blown modern idiom largely as a result of the impact of Cubism on ambitious and impressionable photographers. They ingeniously argued that it was not so much the visual appearance of Cubist works that was influential, but rather the way ideas about Cubism were transmitted through exhibition reviews, the magazine *Camera Work*, and other texts.[16] Although excluded from their argument, the Precisionist artists fit into this general schema. As Friedman wrote of the Precisionists, and photographers could be included as well, they "were synthesizers . . . [they] had less interest in Cubism's abstruse ideology than in pragmatic use of its forms and formulae."[17]

Just as very few photographs of the 1920s resemble Cubist painting, so do few bear similarities to Precisionist painting. Even in instances where Sheeler painted versions of compositions he had first

20. Charles Sheeler. *Cactus and Photographer's Lamp.* 1931. Gelatin silver print, 9½ x 6⅝". The Museum of Modern Art, New York. Gift of Samuel M. Kootz

21. Charles Demuth. *My Egypt.* 1927. Oil on board, 35¾ x 30". Collection Whitney Museum of American Art, New York. Purchase, with funds from Gertrude Vanderbilt Whitney

established in photography, it is the differences rather than the similarities that are striking. It is almost impossible for photography to elide space and detail while maintaining sharpness, and this is among the most important characteristics of Precisionist painting. For instance, Sheeler's painting *Cactus* (plate 104) differs considerably from its source photograph of the same year, *Cactus and Photographer's Lamp* (fig. 20). The painting utilizes a smaller portion of the image than appears in the photograph. Although subdued, color is a vital feature in the painting as it cannot be in the photograph. In addition, the rendering of the painted walls is softer and more tactile than that of the rest of the painting, which is a kind of variation of handling that also cannot occur in photographs. The photo is lively with subtle modulations of light, which are greatly simplified into broad, tonally uniform planes in the painting. Most striking is that Sheeler neglected to represent the prickly pear cactus's spines in the painting, although they are prominent in the photograph.

In the same year as Sheeler made *Criss-Crossed Conveyors*, Charles Demuth painted *My Egypt* (fig. 21). In this work, Demuth's characteristic linear extensions of form into space cause a slight shimmying in the forms of the grain elevators. Not so much Futurist lines of force or Cubist projections as faint flattening and realignment of surface planes, they subtly activate empty space. Photography would be hard pressed to imitate both these qualities and the painting's extreme simplification of form. The irony (affectionate or cynical) apparent in the title is very unlike Strand and Sheeler in their devoted fascination with man-made forms.

Ralston Crawford's photograph of a similar subject, *Buffalo Grain Elevators with Tension Wires* (plate 78), made in about 1938, when he took up photography, is more neutral in tone than Strand's and Sheeler's photographs, but less compressed and complex than Demuth's remarkable painting. Crawford drew, painted, and photographed the massive grain elevators that lined the Buffalo waterfront, allowing several media to share in the development of a single vision (plate 77).

Crawford was trained as a painter; he came to photography later than Outerbridge, Weston, Cunningham, and others who were important presences during the 1920s. Steiner, on the other hand, was first a successful commercial photographer. In 1926 or '27, he met Strand and experienced an epiphany concerning the central importance of impeccable technique in photography. Like Sheeler and Outerbridge, he was represented in the great international *Film und Foto* show of 1929 in Stuttgart.[18] The exhibition celebrated the modernity of the photographic medium, its ties to film and to the fine and applied graphic arts, and its abstract, experimental capabilities. The by-then typical American absorption in photographic technique and print quality was not valued in the vast Stuttgart presentation, from which Strand and Stieglitz were noticeably absent. Steiner's *Portrait of Louis Lozowick* (plate 66) illustrates his affiliation with Lozowick and his circle of machine-form enthusiasts, but he worked in other modes as well. *American Rural Baroque* (plate 122) employs natural lighting in a faintly Cubist manner. It also recalls Sheeler's Bucks County work and predicts the rural documentary photographs made by Walker Evans and others in the 1930s. In 1931, Steiner defended the purity of modern photography in a disparaging review of a photographic compendium published by the Camera Pictorialists of Los Angeles, whose competent execution of standard design formulas came too close to his own pre-Strand work.[19] One of the few photographers included in this selection who escaped Steiner's wrath was Edward Weston.

Already much better known than the *retardataire* provincial amateurs of the Camera Pictorialists of Los Angeles, Weston nonetheless kept faith with them. He had begun as a competent professional portraitist and an enthusiastic amateur practitioner of pictorialism. By 1930, he had assumed the mantle of photographic authority on the West Coast, having even made a pilgrimage to visit Stieglitz in 1922. Although welcomed, he failed to receive Stieglitz's imprimatur as had Strand, and others—perhaps a disciple across the country was less valuable than those close by, on call. But while in New York he formed close ties of mutual admiration with Sheeler. After a sojourn in Mexico City, Weston returned to California.

From 1932 to '35, Weston was the presiding spirit of a photographic association called Group f/64, after a camera aperture setting. The name indicated a purely photographic aesthetic; f/64 specifically denoted the setting most conducive to sharpness of focus throughout a picture's visual field—a specifically antipictorialist program.[20] Other f/64 tenets included the use of the largest camera possible, printing only on glossy papers, never trimming or retouching prints, and displaying prints only on plain white mounts, all intended to maximize and enhance pictorial clarity. Though strongly rooted in the exaltation of technique and craftsmanship, Weston's aesthetic had transcendental aspects as well, reflecting his assimilation of Stieglitz's Symbolist aesthetics.

22. Charles Sheeler. *Wheels*. 1939. Silver print, 6½ x 9½". Courtesy The Museum of Fine Arts, Boston. Gift of William H. and Saundra B. Lane

23. Albert Renger-Patzsch. *Stairwell.* 1929. Gelatin silver print, 9 × 6¾". The Metropolitan Museum of Art, New York. Ford Motor Company Collection, Gift of Ford Motor Company and John C. Waddell, 1987.1100.149

Despite Stieglitz's legacy, Weston's closeness to Sheeler was particularly significant during the 1920s, and their friendship continued into the 1940s. They photographed barns in Connecticut together in 1941, and Weston's *Santa Fe, New York* of that year (plate 85) owes much to Sheeler's *Wheels* (fig. 22). In 1925, when Weston photographed the *Plaster Works* (plate 52), he was experimenting with atypical subject matter that brought him much closer to Sheeler and Precisionism. Best known for sensual nudes, sculptural still lifes, and coastal landscapes, Weston photographed the plaster works as a series of radiant planes rather than a comprehensible factory. To Weston, the beauty of a machine, smokestack, or factory lay purely in its form, part of the universal harmony available for apprehension by eye or camera. He had no interest in industrial motifs for their own sake, and stood aloof from the Eastern and European tendencies to integrate artistic and commercial photography. The near infinite reproducibility of photography in mass media held few charms for one who believed that the central task of the photographer was the production of fine-art works by hand.

Despite this doctrine, Weston served as a consultant for the *Film und Foto* exhibition, sending examples of the work of San Francisco–area photographer Imogen Cunningham as well as his own. They shared the West Coast romantic preference for natural subjects, which put them somewhat at odds with the "new objectivity" of German and European photography. László Moholy-Nagy, who arranged the first room of the Stuttgart show, filled it with anonymous photographs including advertising and scientific images. Nearer to stylized abstraction in composition than to Cubism, Dada, or Constructivist photomontage, Weston's and Cunningham's photographs nonetheless showed a clarity of form that impressed the Europeans and was congruent with their work.

Cunningham's *Shredded Wheat Tower* and *Fageol Ventilators* (plates 62, 72) are exceptional among her oeuvre, in which plant studies and portraits are most numerous. Her career has certain parallels with that of Elsie Driggs, who also worked in many manners and won acclaim late in a long life after important early avant-garde work. Marginalized in part because of geography and perhaps also because of gender, Cunningham produced some of the most sophisticated photographic abstractions of the period. *Shredded Wheat Tower* is closer to the European vision than anything done by an American photographer previously. The simplicity of mechanical forms composed as abstraction against white sky from a seemingly perspectiveless angle of view, is close in spirit to the clean, remote exactitude of Albert Renger-Patzsch's *Stairwell* (fig. 23).

Such photographs recall Martin Friedman's point that the essential characteristic of Precisionist painting is attraction to "the colossal geometry of the city and industry. In Precisionist paintings of skyscrapers, bridges, factories, and docks, all traces of damage or decay disappeared, specific architectural details were simplified, and these forms were recast as the proud symbols of technological splendor."[21] Attaining freedom from signs of decay was more difficult for photographers than for painters, which partially explains Cunningham's and Weston's normal preference for the more easily rendered perfections of natural forms over those of industry.

As both pictorialism and Stieglitz's second style of Expressionistic abstraction gave way to the decorative stylization so compatible with commercial photography in New York, across the Atlantic a laboratory model of photographic experimentation arose in Germany and the Soviet Union, reshaping the design emphases of pictorialism into a bold modern language. Photographic authority was displaced from a single figure to various individuals, doctrines, and locations across the United States and around the world. Strand photographed throughout the world from a base in France, and Sheeler moved away from photography somewhat in his later years. Walker Evans and Berenice Abbott, not to mention the many photographers of the FSA (Farm Security Administration) project, worked in various regions directing their energies toward clarifying photography's role as a documentary rather than a fine-art medium. Weston and his f/64 colleague Ansel Adams continued to practice purist craftsmanship and to pursue expressive form in photography. Working in the American West, they preserved a photographic tradition that came to be regarded as central, inevitable, and official in part through the backing of powerful presences like the new Museum of Modern Art. The stature gained by this branch of American photography has served to deflect the attention of historians from more complex, ambiguous, or even contradictory episodes in photographic modernism, such as the medium's intersections with Precisionism.

PRECISIONISM AND THE CAMERA

It is unusual to speak of a Precisionist photography as one might, for instance, of Precisionist drawing or printmaking. Nevertheless, it does not make sense to speak of Precisionism without considering photography—for all that no Precisionist painting or drawing looks much like a photograph when scale, color, surface texture, and degree of detail are the criteria of comparison. The terms "Immaculate" and "Precisionist" in some cases are even more descriptive of photography than of painting—how well both apply to Strand's *Akeley* and Sheeler's *Criss-Crossed Conveyors*! Many of Precisionism's traits are shared to some extent with most photography. The analogies between Precisionism and photography lie not so much in the adoption of the characteristic look of photographs as in popular ideas about photography: that it is modern, technical, objective, hard-edged—in short, *precise*. The coincidence of both modern industrial and rural vernacular subject matter in photography and painting cements the connection.

Both the history of photography and that of painting address the rise of American avant-garde styles separate from but equal to those in Europe during the 1920s, the introduction of industrial motifs, and the relation of abstraction to a continuing representationalism in these works. Photography was then coming to prominence as the first art medium in which Americans assumed leadership in the international arts community. But any narrative concerning the loose group of individuals identified as the Precisionists differs substantially from the stories generally told about photographers and photography during this period. For much of the first half of the twentieth century, American photographers and their chroniclers have emphasized simplified, unitary accounts of the medium, a strategy very different from that of the history of modernist painting, which catalogues the many (often simultaneous and overlapping) different groups, movements, tendencies, and isms.

It may be in the realm of film, not still photography, that we find the most perfect extension of Precisionist thinking into camera art. Perhaps, indeed, it is in film that we find the ultimate example of the Precisionist style, in Sheeler and Strand's *Manhatta*. In that film, urban and machine imagery expresses the tensions between detailed precise rendering, Cubist stylization, and simplified abstraction more vividly than in any photograph or painting. In *Manhatta*, an entire city "pictorializes," as Frank Lloyd Wright put it, offering itself to the artist and thus to the viewer, as a work of art. Reality renders itself as art—immaculate, precise, intensified, absolute, American, and urban.

NOTES

1. Quoted in Constance Rourke, *Charles Sheeler: Artist in the American Tradition* (New York: Harcourt Brace and Company, 1938), p. 119.
2. Paul Strand, "Photography," *Seven Arts,* August 1917, p. 524.
3. Marius de Zayas, "Modern Art: The Theories and Representation," *Camera Work,* vol. 44, October 1913, p. 13.
4. Charles Sheeler, "Recent Photographs by Alfred Stieglitz," *The Arts,* vol. 3, May 1923, p. 345.
5. Francis Picabia, "A Post-Cubist's Impression of New York," *The New York Tribune*, March 9, 1913, part 2, p. 1.
6. Marius de Zayas, "How, When and Why Modern Art Came to New York" (1940s?), published with an introduction and notes by Francis Naumann, *Arts Magazine,* vol. 54, April 1980, p. 104.
7. Frank Lloyd Wright, "The Tyranny of the Skyscraper," *Creative Art,* vol. 8, May 1931, p. 332.
8. The definitive study of *Manhatta* to date is Jan-Christopher Horak's "Modernist Perspectives and Romantic Desire: *Manhatta,*" *Afterimage,* November 1987, pp. 8–15, which masterfully charts fluctuations between modernist and romantic impulses in the film. *Manhatta* was shown at the Rialto Theater on Broadway as *New York the Magnificent* for one week in July 1921, at a Dadaist soirée in Paris in 1922 as *Fumée de New York,* and at the London Film Society in 1927 as *Manhatta.*
9. Paul Strand, press release for *Manhatta,* typescript copy, Department of Film, The Museum of Modern Art, New York.
10. Harold Clurman, "Photographs of Paul Strand," *Creative Art,* vol. 5, October 1929, p. 735.
11. In *Charles Sheeler: The Photographs*, exh. cat. (Boston: Museum of Fine Arts, 1987), Theodore Stebbins and Norman Keyes briefly suggest that the traditional dates ranging from 1914 to 1917 for many of Sheeler's Bucks County photographs are implausible and prefer to date all of them to 1917. As they offer no clear proof, it is impossible to accept their argument without further evidence or debate. Constance Rourke, the author of the earliest comprehensive account of Sheeler's work, does not reproduce or discuss his photographs. Martin Friedman dates this photograph, which he titles *Pennsylvania Barn* to 1915 (Martin Friedman, *Charles Sheeler* [New York: Watson Guptill Publications, 1975]). Beaumont Newhall's authoritative *The History of Photography* (New York: The Museum of Modern Art, 1982) titled the picture *Bucks County Barn* and dated it 1916.
12. Quoted in Henry M. Sayre, "American Vernacular: Objectivism, Precisionism, and the Aesthetics of the Machine," *Twentieth-Century Literature,* vol. 35, Fall 1989, p. 313.
13. Paul Strand, "Photography and the New God," *Broom,* vol. 3, no. 4, August 1922, p. 252.
14. Charles Sheeler, quoted in Rourke, p. 130.
15. "By Their Works Ye Shall Know Them," *Vanity Fair,* February 1928, p. 62. For the relations between Sheeler's commercial and fine art work in the context of the Ford photographs, see Susan Fillen-Yeh, "Charles Sheeler: Industry, Fashion, and the Vanguard," *Arts,* vol. 54, February 1980, pp. 154–58.
16. John Pultz and Catherine B. Scallen, *Cubism and American Photography, 1910–1930,* exh. cat. (Williamstown: Sterling and Francine Clark Institute, 1981), pp. 16–17.
17. Martin L. Friedman, *The Precisionist View in American Art*, exh. cat. (Minneapolis: Walker Art Center, 1960), p. 22.
18. The best brief account of *Film und Foto* in context (in English) is by Christopher Phillips in Maria Morris Hambourg, *The New Vision: Photography Between the Wars* (New York: The Metropolitan Museum of Art, 1989), pp. 65–108.
19. Ralph Steiner, review of *The Pictorialist, Creative Art,* vol. 8, May 1931, p. 381.
20. John Paul Edwards, "Group f/64," *Camera Craft,* March 1935, pp. 107–8, 110, 112–13.
21. Friedman, p. 28.

INSPIRED BY SCIENCE AND THE MODERN:
Precisionism and American Culture

Miles Orvell

WE CANNOT DATE WITH exactness the beginning of "modern" culture in America, but surely it was heralded in the most exalted terms as early as 1871, in Walt Whitman's prophetic *Democratic Vistas*: "America demands a poetry that is bold, modern, and all-surrounding and kosmical, as she is herself. It must in no respect ignore science or the modern, but inspire itself with science and the modern. It must bend its vision toward the future, more than the past."[1] "Science and the modern": the two were firmly linked in Whitman's forward-looking vision in a marriage that captured the post–Civil War optimism of American civilization. Yet Whitman's demand for an art that would be commensurate with science and the modern went virtually unanswered until the first decades of the twentieth century, when a group of artists—among them the "Precisionists"—at last began to create a visual and literary culture that responded to the extraordinary transformations of American society under the impact of the machine. But when it arrived, this new world, and the art it inspired, was in some ways far different from what Whitman might have envisioned. For Whitman, it was a matter of incorporating the world of science and technology into a larger aesthetic vision of democratic civilization; for the modernists the new world of the machine became far more compelling, and in some ways far more threatening, to behold. An early sign of things to come is visible in the response of Henry Adams, who, gazing at the huge generating dynamos at the Chicago Exposition in 1893—large beyond a scale imagined by Whitman—saw in them, with awe and some dread, a symbol of the age's most powerful cultural force, occupying a position as central to our society as the Virgin had for medieval culture.[2]

By any measure, the changes during the decades following Whitman's pronouncement of 1871 constituted virtually a rebuilding of the material world, placing the human subject in an environment that was quickly expanding beyond his or her understanding: not candles or oil in a lamp to light the room, but lightbulbs powered by electricity, fed into the house by wires; not the book or the stereographic card in the parlor, but the wireless radio. In the home, as David Nye points out, specialized industrial processes had been in effect since the 1880s, but with electricity mechanization was much accelerated. In 1910, one in ten urban homes had electricity; by 1930, most did, and the consumer was surrounded with new machines—irons, sewing machines, vacuum cleaners, toasters, washing machines, refrigerators—and the household was transformed into a mechanized environment.[3]

If domestic space was changing rapidly as a result of technology during the early twentieth century, the workplace was changing even more, with dramatically increasing productivity and equally increasing regimentation of the worker. The use of electrically powered machines in factories grew from five percent of total horsepower in 1899 to over eighty percent in 1929. The efficiency with which natural resources were used also grew, along with a markedly increased rate of productivity, especially in the years after World War I.[4] While mechanization was lowering the prices of consumer goods, it was raising the cost to the worker producing them, at least in physical terms: the factory, under the influence of Frederick Winslow Taylor, was increasingly regimenting the worker's movements in coordination with the requirements of the new productive techniques; driven by the goal of maximum efficiency, the new science of factory management meant increased production along with increased surveillance and increased exhaustion for the worker.[5] For the office worker, too, interactions with the machine—whether telephone, adding machine, or typewriter—enforced a rhythm of repetition and fine coordination.

Outside the home and the workplace, technology was transforming the nature of space, shrinking distances that had once seemed vast and expanding the size of cities that had once seemed scaled to human dimensions. The railroad had, by the end of the nineteenth century, created a network of interconnected routes assuring the servicing of commercial markets across the United States. And commuter rails had extended the city beyond its nineteenth century core to expanded metropolitan regions, embracing suburban communities that became bedrooms to the city's commercial districts.[6] After 1900, the automobile—one of the major products of America's manufacturing system—was rolling off the assembly lines in ever-increasing numbers: from four thousand in 1900 to over four million in 1929. During the same years, surfaced roads increased from one hundred fifty thousand miles in 1904 to nearly seven hundred thousand miles in 1930.

Cities grew outward, expanding into suburban regions, and they grew upward, from their pre-elevator six stories to the neck-bending heights of the modern skyscraper. Early experiments in framed iron construction, using diagonal bracing, had begun in the 1880s in Chicago and New York and were raising the height of the urban building to eight, ten, fifteen stories tall. (The steam and hydraulic elevator, followed around the turn of the century by the electric safety elevator, made it possible to use these tall buildings as office space.) As the height grew to twenty stories, the masonry walls were eliminated in favor of glass curtain walls, and before the end of the century the skyscraper had pushed as high as thirty stories.[7] The tallest building in its time, Daniel Burnham's triangular Flatiron Building of 1903 in Manhattan soon became the subject of some notable photographs by Alvin Langdon Coburn, Alfred Stieglitz, and Edward Steichen, who were among the first to feature the new skyscrapers in a purely aesthetic context. Gradually, as the New York skyline changed, the great buildings of the early twentieth century—the Beaux-Arts Singer Building, 1906–8, and the Gothicized Woolworth Building, 1911–13, followed by the exuberantly Art Deco Chrysler Building, 1929–31 (plates 28, 32) and the more restrained Empire State Building, 1928–31 (plate 30)—would become icons of the modern age, their advertising function as symbols of corporate power soon transformed into more generalized symbols of modern industrial civilization. By the 1920s, their geometric forms were inspiring a range of treatments, from the detailed to the simplified, from the objective to the subjective, and in a variety of media.

But why, during this period of revolutionary change, did it take so long for Whitman's demand to be answered? Why were the arts in general so removed from these transformations in American society? One reason is that the very things that had so excited Whitman—the iron foundries, the tall buildings, the manufactured products displayed in the shop windows, the sailing ships, the steam engines—were generally seen to exist in a totally separate sphere from the world of "art."[8] Art, within the sanctioned boundaries of the academy and the library and within the pages of such family parlor magazines as *The Atlantic, Scribner's,* and *Harper's,* was idealizing and inspirational, a matter of lofty sentiments and lovely forms—flowers, butterflies, teacups, and peacock feathers. Art was, indeed, one of the primary defenses *against* the world outside the parlor—the world of steam engines, railroads, bridges, iron girders, and factories. If the machine was going to be seen publicly, it would have to be dressed up for the occasion like some exotic primitive, the naked functionalism of a steam engine or a sewing machine clothed in a decorative embellishment of vine leaves or classical columns or symbolic figures. The Brooklyn Bridge itself, that monument to engineering genius built in 1869–83, had to be clothed in Gothic arches (plate 26). Americans were learning to live with the machine, but only gradually. Only in the design of factory machinery—that is, where public reception was obviously insignificant, where function alone mattered—do we find the nineteenth century developing the stripped-down functionalist look; and only after the turn of the century does the vernacular simplicity of purely utilitarian forms begin to appear in the industrial landscape—factories, grain elevators, and eventually oil tanks.[9]

Yet precisely here, in the machinery and architectural forms of the industrial landscape, did the new modernist vocabulary find its inspiration and did science and the modern as a result begin to find its way into the culture at large. When Marcel Duchamp and Francis Picabia came to America, they enthusiastically embraced the vocabulary of "the modern"—mechanical forms, elaborately contrived mechanisms, readymades—with a light, metaphorical touch. This opened the way for American artists, in turn, to look at the new subject matter of the city and the machine and to see how the new vision of Cubism could be joined to technology and still be consonant with American values and traditions.

The American response was not simply a wholehearted embrace of the new (as it was for the Italian Futurists); it was significantly tempered by an effort to connect the new age of the machine with some cultural tradition that would give it sanction. The search for the new was accompanied by a backward look, a retrospective yearning to identify with the nineteenth-century past; one finds it in Cather, Eliot, Faulkner, Williams, Fitzgerald, and in the intellectuals peripheral to the Precisionist movement, Van Wyck Brooks and Lewis Mumford. For the Precisionist movement especially, a central cultural icon of nineteenth-century America was Whitman. Certainly it was fitting that he should assist this new accommodation to science and the modern, fifty years after having demanded it. Whitman would become one of the cornerstones of the "usable past" that the first generation of American modernists were looking for, and he was treated accordingly by Brooks in his 1915 volume, *America's Coming of Age,* as a synthesis in American culture of the opposite poles of theory and action, idealism and business. And it was precisely in terms of Whitman that Paul Rosenfeld, in 1921, celebrated Stieglitz, whose "subjugation of the complex modern mechanism" of the camera was portrayed as the potential salvation of the United States, "the land most ravished by mechanical civilization." He continued, "Save for Whitman, there has been amongst us no native-born artist equal to this photographer."[10]

In short, the task of incorporating the modern into American art was a process of opening up a critique of America in terms of its prevailing industrial civilization. To the European, America was a rich, ebullient enfant terrible, a quirky child filled with primitive energy. The American artist was usually more serious, more ambivalent, more worried about the ravages of mechanical civilization. What made Stieglitz such a central figure to this generation of modernists was his symbolic role within the art world: he was, as a photographer, the master of the quintessentially modern machine, the camera. As Paul Strand observed, Stieglitz established "spiritual control over a machine" and thus offered the model for modern civilization.[11]

In the hands of the modern artist, the camera was functioning as an instrument for reforming perception, a way of relating the new vision to technology and art, which became the foundation of Precisionism and of the American contribution to international modernism. Technology became a creative force for the artist by being defined as a new "screen" or "filter" through which the world was experienced: Jean Epstein, writing for *Broom* in 1922, observed, "all these instruments: telephone, microscope, magnifying glass, cinematograph, lens, microphone, gramophone, automobile, kodak, aeroplane, are not merely dead objects. [These] machines become part of ourselves, interposing themselves between the world and us, filtering reality as the screen filters radium emanations. Thanks to them we have no longer a simple, clear, continuous, constant notion of an object. . . . The world for people today is like descriptive geometry, with its infinite planes of projection."[12] Epstein's formulation is almost literally illustrated in some of Charles Demuth's paintings, such as *My Egypt* (fig. 21), where the architectural image is overlaid with a screen of fractured lines and geometric shapes.

Behind the idolization of the camera was the more general goal of ending the seeming hostility between science and art. In 1927, Jane Heap, in the issue of *The Little Review* that served as the catalogue for the *Machine-Age Exposition,* affirmed, "There is a great new race of men in America: the Engineer. He has created a new mechanical world, . . . it is inevitable and important to the civilization of today that he make a union with the architect and artist. This affiliation will . . . end the immense waste in each domain and will become a new creative force."[13]

One of the clearest expressions of this characteristic definition from within the Precisionist movement appears in Louis Lozowick's "The Americanization of Art" (see Appendix). Lozowick reads the history of America as "a history of gigantic engineering feats and colossal mechanical construction." He goes on to argue—echoing Whitman—that the American environment—skyscrapers, grain elevators, steel mills, oil wells, copper mines, lumber yards—is "not in itself art but only raw material which becomes art when reconstructed by the artist according to the requirement of aesthetic form."

Lozowick's own prints best exemplify this goal. Emphasizing the geometric forms of the industrial landscape and the city of skyscrapers, Lozowick's angle of vision exploits the drama of scale—looking up at the massive girders of bridges or at huge cylindrical gas tanks, or looking down on the massed forms of buildings. Surrounding the static industrial structures are moving automobiles, airplanes, an occasional pedestrian. The scene takes place in a moment in history: Lozowick's world is in motion.

Not so with Charles Sheeler, whose work is far more a meditation on shapes and form that removes the object from the realm of history and time. It is in Sheeler that Precisionism finds its most powerful and in some ways its most enigmatic figure. For Sheeler the *construction* of the image is of paramount interest, just as it is the construction of material things that interests him as subject matter. One can see Sheeler in 1920 paring away the ornament from his painted skyscrapers, turning them into the stripped-down functionalist forms they would in fact become later in the decade (as, for example, in Howe and Lescaze's Philadelphia Savings Fund Society Building, 1929–32, or Raymond Hood's New York McGraw-Hill Building, 1931). Sheeler quickly learned to exploit the distortions of mechanical seeing, resulting in a variety of paintings in which the subject was seen through the close-up (*Upper Deck* [fig. 10], *Yankee Clipper* [plate 85]), the reflection (*Self-Portrait*, 1923, The Museum of Modern Art, New York), or the distorted juxtaposition (*American Interior* [plate 127]). The camera anchored Sheeler in perceptual realism, giving his depictions of the object a three-dimensional solidity at the same time that he exploited its distorting vision.

The new camera-vision is fully evident as early as 1921, in the film that Sheeler made with Strand, *Manhatta*. It is notable for its clear demonstration of the importance of Whitman to the modern artist, for the film is intercut with titles drawn from several of his poems, the particular lines serving as thematic headings for the visual imagery. Ironically, however, it is as if the prophet of science and the modern were now being used to soften the effect of the actual modern city, a city that as pictured is far beyond what even Whitman might have imagined.

Sheeler's engagement with science and the modern reaches its most complex and ambiguous state in the photographs he made at Henry Ford's River Rouge plant and the paintings that followed. In the Rouge paintings he created a series of icons of American industry that have been read as celebrations of Ford and American capitalism. But there is more to the series than at first meets the eye, and understanding Sheeler's place within the discourse of modernism requires looking closely at the work and at the subject, the Ford factory.

The Rouge factory, designed to build the new Model A that was replacing the outmoded Model T, was an industrial city on a scale far greater than Ford's old Highland plant and far greater than anything previously conceived (plate 64). With twenty-three main buildings, seventy lesser structures, ninety-three miles of railroad tracks, fifty-three thousand machines, and seventy-five thousand employees, it was a site for production that began with raw materials to create steel and ended with cars. The man behind this enterprise was, at the time, among the most celebrated in the world, his mythical dimension having far outstripped his humble self. To Ford, the goal was the constant perfection of the manufacturing process, not the constant innovation of the finished product. Starting with the best possible functional design of the automobile, Ford shaped around it the organization of the factory and the merchandising of its products. With efficiency the primary virtue, all waste—excess weight in the vehicle, unused by-products created in the process—were to be eliminated. Waste was also excess force used by the worker in performing the job, and Ford subscribed to Taylor's principles of "Scientific Management," matching the man to the machine and the machine to the man in as perfect a wedding as possible. Of course perfection in this regard might mean the robotization of human functions to nearly insufferable degrees. Chaplin's crazed tramp on the assembly line in *Modern Times*, 1936, is perhaps the most famous image of somatic dysfunction, his finely tuned movements repeated to the point where he himself becomes a lunatic automaton.

24. Charles Sheeler. *American Landscape.* 1931. Oil on canvas, 24 x 31". The Museum of Modern Art, New York. Gift of Abby Aldrich Rockefeller

What is striking about the series Sheeler did in 1927 is the complete absence of the famous assembly line and the nearly complete absence of the worker from the scene of production (plates 54–57). Instead Sheeler shows us the exteriors and interiors of buildings that carry the manufacturing process along, concentrating for the most part on the production of steel from raw materials and omitting the later stages of car production. "My program as mapped out now," Sheeler wrote to Walter Arensberg, "will consist of photographs of details of the plants and portraits of machinery as well as the new Ford (take my word and order one now) and also the Lincoln."[14] (Sheeler took his own advice and bought himself a Lincoln, with great pleasure.) Deliberately concealing the harsh reality of assembly-line production, Sheeler emphasizes instead the mystery of the machine, dramatizing the abstract geometric shapes, the intricacy of overhead lines and conveyor belts, the massive shapes of huge presses, generators, and rail carriers. In a way, Sheeler is sustaining, though revising, the nineteenth-century relationship between technology and art, maintaining the purity of the artwork as a defense against the severities of industrial life, but doing so, paradoxically, by aestheticizing industry. Further, Sheeler creates an experience of the technologically sublime, the awesome power of the machine when viewed as a creative force, so overpowering as to be slightly terrifying. Where human beings do appear they seem dwarfed by the giant machinery, purely ancillary to the kettles, furnaces, ladles, and dynamos they serve. The world of Ford according to Sheeler was essentially an aesthetic universe of calm and order, worlds away from the description of the Rouge factory in even so adulatory a biography as William Stidger's of 1923, where the author is reminded of Rembrandt and of hell: "Down the incline we went . . . to the foundries where great molten kettles of white-hot iron were swinging on great runways propelled by . . . men, who in the blare and glare of splashing, simmering, smoldering iron, open furnaces with streams of molten, running iron, look like figures from some grim, Rembrandt picture."[15]

Sheeler went even further than Stidger when he wrote for the March 1931 issue of the new *Fortune* magazine, in which his *American Landscape* (fig. 24) was reproduced: "[At the Ford plant] is to be seen the machine working with an infallibility which precludes human competition. Noticeable is the absence of debris. Everything in the path of the activity is in the process of being utilized; . . . one is witnessing the workings of an absolute monarchy. It confirms a preference for that type of government with the proviso that the monarch be of the calibre of Henry Ford."[16]

Ford's virtues of order, efficiency, and managerial expertise had widespread popular appeal, especially during the teens and twenties, when Progressive intellectuals like Walter Lippmann and Herbert Croly looked to a disinterested managerial elite to solve the problems of government, with Ford and industry as a model. These utopian ideals would flourish briefly in the Technocracy movement of the Depression, as a reaction to the proven disorder of the marketplace. If Sheeler's response to Ford—forgetting the labor practices, the strikes, the Ford police, the social campaigns—was thus a positive one, it was not far from the popular response to the myth of Ford.[17]

25. Charles Sheeler. *Industry.* 1932, from negatives of Ford River Rouge factory taken in 1927. Silver gelatin print triptych, 8 x 28". The Art Institute of Chicago. Julien Levy Collection, Gift of Jean and Julien Levy, 1975.1146a-c

Perhaps the clearest icon of Precisionism (and of Ford) is Sheeler's photographic triptych *Industry* (fig. 25), made for a 1932 exhibition of proposed murals at The Museum of Modern Art, New York. Sheeler used several preexisting Rouge photographs for this work: the narrow side panels are taken from *Stamping Press,* 1927, divided vertically, while the central image uses *Criss-Crossed Conveyors* (plate 57), with a background composed of the smokestacks of *Power House No. 1,* 1927, and a reverse image of *Pulverizer Building* (plate 55). The triptych is interesting as a formal composition and a conceptual play of opposites: the two side panels break apart the single image, while the central panel puts together three images. Thus Sheeler's artistic process imitates the industrial process of breaking down raw materials and synthesizing components into a new whole. In effect, the *Industry* triptych is a *conceptual* work; the *idea* of the work is an essential component of our understanding; it is not just a representation of machinery and it is not just a play of forms.

In fact, we need to look at Sheeler's work generally more as conceptual art than as formalistic construction. Sheeler's paintings of the Ford plant are no less interesting in this regard. In each case, Sheeler depicts with "photographic realism" scenes that are based on his earlier photographs of the industrial plant. But all three can be seen as conceptual works, where an opposition is crucial to the motive—an opposition between the title and the image that establishes an irony. Yes, this is the new world, but it is a new world that is evoked in terms of what is not there. *Classic Landscape* (plate 65) is conceived along "classic" lines: Sheeler depicts silos of a cement plant (the equivalent of classical columns) in the middle ground, while the rail tracks carry us from the foreground to the right side of the picture, to a sharply vanishing point. But it is devoid of the human presence and human scale, which were at the center of classical civilization. In *American Landscape,* nature has been coerced into the industrial scheme: the water reflects the industrial structures, the sky takes its clouds from the smokestack. All of these paintings have been taken as analytic representations of the "new world" of industrial America, a world of order and productivity; yet I believe they represent an ironic commentary on this new world, as close to "social comment" as Sheeler cared to come.[18]

26. Charles Sheeler. *Walt Whitman Relics.* 1944. Gelatin silver print, 7 9/16 x 9 1/2". The Museum of Modern Art, New York. Gift of the photographer

At the heart of the machine age lay a division of labor and a division of society between those who worked with their hands and those who worked with their heads. The American industrial system as conceived by Ford and Taylor believed these divisions to be eternally right. But Ford's utopia of the factory conceals a division within the individual, between the head and the hand, a division that all art tends to heal. It may be no accident that both Ford and Sheeler were deeply fascinated by the crafts of preindustrial America, as if for both of them, so equally immersed in the machine, it was essential to keep the spiritual and cultural ideal in constant view: the production of hand-made goods that resulted from the joining of hand and head. You couldn't go back to that earlier time, they both knew. But you couldn't forget it, either. So Ford created his Greenfield Village, filled with hand-made antiques and folk objects; and Sheeler—while immersed in the imagery of technology and the city—was also deeply involved with the aesthetic of Shaker craft, and many of his paintings reflect the integration of hand and head that is embodied in these nineteenth-century artifacts, not to mention their preindustrial functionalist form.

These paradoxes persist: in 1944, as World War II was reaching its climax, America's premiere business magazine, *Fortune,* commissioned Sheeler to do a series of still-life photographs related to great nineteenth-century American cultural figures. *Walt Whitman Relics* (fig. 26) includes books, photographs, and memorabilia (from the collection of the Houghton Library, Harvard University) relating to Whitman, displayed in the manner of a nineteenth century rack picture, including a tabletop arrangement such as William Harnett might have painted. Whitman again: "America demands a poetry that must . . . inspire itself with science and the modern." The modernist movement, including the Precisionists, was precisely an effort to answer that call for a bold art equal to the country itself; but by the time the artist had moved science and the modern from outside the discourse of art to inside, technology had come to seem not only a defining attribute of American culture, but a dangerously dominating one. And Whitman, once sounding the barbaric yawp that was so offensive to the genteel tradition, had become himself a safe part of that tradition, as Sheeler reconceived it. Whitman became for one of the preeminent modernists a symbol of both the modern and the past, and of that moment of optimism when the vistas of American democracy seemed happily created by the forces of industry and technology. Inspired by science and the modern, the artist of the twentieth century would find himself or herself climbing the ladder that Sheeler painted in *American Landscape*; the ladder is unoccupied, but one imagines the modern artist on it—one foot on the salvage ship, the other lifting up into the air above it, seeking perhaps a vantage point from which to assess the scene, a point both inside and outside of it.

NOTES

1. Walt Whitman, *Democratic Vistas* (1871), in *Leaves of Grass and Selected Prose by Walt Whitman*, ed. John Kouwenhoven (New York: The Modern Library, 1950), p. 503.
2. Henry Adams, "The Dynamo and the Virgin," *The Education of Henry Adams* (1918; New York: Random House, 1931).
3. David E. Nye, *Electrifying America: Social Meanings of a New Technology* (Cambridge, Massachusetts: The MIT Press, 1990), p. 239.
4. Nathan Rosenberg, *Technology and American Economic Growth* (White Plains: M.E. Sharpe, 1972), pp. 162–63.
5. See Hugh G. J. Aitken, *Scientific Management in Action: Taylorism at Watertown Arsenal, 1908–1915* (Princeton: Princeton University Press, 1985).
6. Kenneth T. Jackson, *Crabgrass Frontier: The Suburbanization of the United States* (New York: Oxford, 1985).
7. Carl Condit, *American Building: Materials and Techniques from the First Colonial Settlements to the Present* (Chicago: University of Chicago Press, 1968), pp. 15–20.
8. See John F. Kasson, "The Aesthetics of Machinery," in *Civilizing the Machine: Technology and Republican Values in America, 1776–1900* (New York: Grossman, 1976) pp. 139–80.
9. See John A. Kouwenhoven, *The Arts in Modern American Civilization* (New York: W.W. Norton, 1948), pp. 12–42, 204–9.
10. Paul Rosenfeld, "Stieglitz," *The Dial*, vol. 70, April 1921, reprinted in Beaumont Newhall, ed., *Photography: Essays and Images* (New York and Boston: The Museum of Modern Art and New York Graphic Society, 1980), pp. 214, 215.
11. Paul Strand, "Photography and the New God," *Broom*, vol. 3, 1922, reprinted in Alan Trachtenberg, ed., *Classic Essays on Photography* (New Haven: Leete's Island Books, 1980), p. 151.
12. Jean Epstein, "The New Conditions of Literary Phenomena," *Broom*, vol. 2, April 1922, pp. 6–7.
13. Jane Heap, "Machine-Age Exposition," *The Little Review*, Spring supplement 1927, p. 36.
14. Charles Sheeler, letter to Walter Arensberg, October 25, 1927, Arensberg Archives. Quoted in Theodore E. Stebbins Jr. and Norman Keyes Jr., *Charles Sheeler: The Photographs*, exh. cat. (Boston: Museum of Fine Arts, 1987), p. 26.
15. William L. Stidger, *Henry Ford: The Man and His Motives* (New York: George H. Doran Company, 1993), p. 114.
16. Charles Sheeler, "Section of the Ford Plant at Dearborn, Michigan," *Fortune*, March 1931, p. 57.
17. Karen Lucic, *Charles Sheeler and the Cult of the Machine* (Cambridge, Massachusetts: Harvard University Press, 1989), pp. 79–80. For a discussion of Ford labor practices see Terry Smith, *Making the Modern: Industry, Art, and Design in America* (Chicago: The University of Chicago Press, 1993), pp. 15–55.
18. Sheeler avowed in an interview in 1954, "I don't believe I could ever indulge in social comment," and then added, "Maybe industry is our great image that lights up the sky. . . . The thing I deplore is the absence of spiritual content." Quoted in Lucic, p. 108.

AMÉRICANISME/AMERIKANISMUS:
The Adventures of a European Myth

Romy Golan

HARD-EDGE EXECUTION, IMPECCABLE delineation of form, sanitized space, utter silence—all qualities one may associate with the term "Precisionism"—describe much of the art produced in France, Weimar Germany, Soviet Russia, and Fascist Italy in the 1920s. Yet American Precisionism had no following in Europe; indeed it drew little attention there. On the contrary, America itself seized the European imagination as the ultimate symbol of modernity. In the aftermath of World War I, as it moved politically and economically to center stage as a global power, America achieved an almost mythical significance for a Europe whose physical, social, and political foundations had been shaken by war and revolution. To people whose sense of history was now qualified by before and after, America represented a "brave new world," a country without history, a nation untouched by war or revolution and thus intact. And thanks to its embrace of Taylorism and Fordism it seemed not only a model of industrial efficiency but a true exemplar of the machine ideology of the future. It served as a distorting mirror on which Europeans could project their hopes and fantasies, their fears and obsessions.

As the Marxist philosopher Antonio Gramsci rightly observed concerning the impact of America and Fordism in the late twenties, the farther East one looked in Europe (that is, Germany and the Soviet Union) the more intense was the cult of Americanism. And yet the fascination with America was first expressed and nurtured by the French. Its prelude can be traced to the activities of Marcel Duchamp, Francis Picabia, Albert Gleizes, and Jean Crotti in New York in 1915.

As the art worlds of Paris and Berlin came to a near standstill from 1914 to 1918, these artists' association with such American counterparts as Alfred Stieglitz, Morton Schamberg, and Louise and Walter Arensberg shifted the focus of the avant-garde for the first time from Europe to New York. The main ideas Duchamp elaborated there had already concerned him in Paris and Munich. But New York, and America in general, acted as an important catalyst for the ultimate conceptualization of his work, which revolved around what would become the two key attributes of Americanism: the machine and mass-production. It was soon after his arrival in New York that Duchamp began work on his magnum opus, *The Large Glass* (fig. 1). Although the famously unfortunate saga of his two sets of dysfunctional apparatuses condemned them to remain forever "bachelor machines," Duchamp's *Large Glass* gave birth, by osmosis, to the most interesting work of New York Dada: Schamberg's pioneering, Precisionist paintings of machines and the more cryptic, ironic, mechanomorphic portraits of Stieglitz, Marius de Zayas, and Picabia (plate 1). He had this to say in an interview conducted in Duchamp's New York apartment in

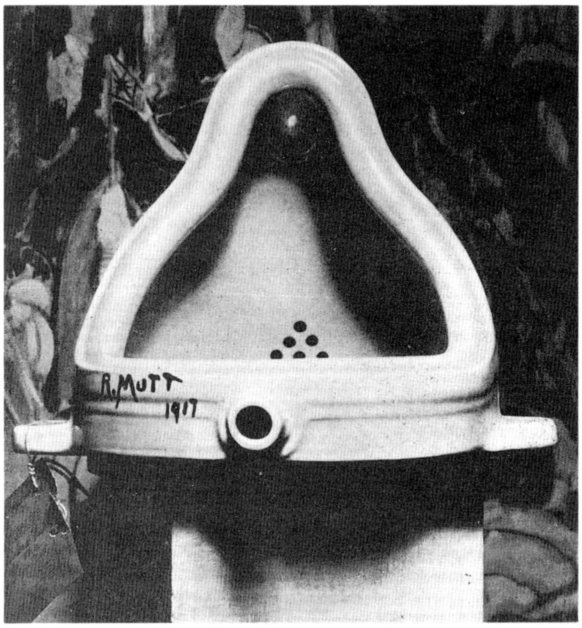

27. Marcel Duchamp. *Fountain*. 1917. Philadelphia Museum of Art. Louise and Walter Arensberg Collection, Arensberg Archives, Francis Bacon Library. Photograph by Alfred Stieglitz reproduced in *The Blind Man*, no. 2, May 1917, p. 4

1915: "This visit to America has brought about a complete revolution in my methods of work. . . . Almost immediately upon coming to America it flashed on me that the genius of the modern world is in machinery and that through machinery art ought to find a most vivid expression."[1]

It was also in New York, thanks to the free-for-all jargon of the garment industry, that Duchamp found a name, Readymade, for his manufactured objects turned art. Having considered using the world's tallest skyscraper, the Woolworth Building, as his first American Readymade, Duchamp settled instead on a porcelain-lipped urinal for his contribution to the Society of Independent Artists exhibition in 1917 (fig. 27).[2] Facing the photograph of the urinal captioned "Fountain by R. Mutt" in the Dada review *Blindman* came the following much-quoted statement by Duchamp on American culture: "Mr. Mutt's Fountain is not immoral, that is absurd. . . . It is a fixture that you see every day in plumbers' show windows. As for plumbing, that is absurd. The only works of art America has given us are her plumbing and her bridges."[3]

By 1918, similar pronouncements would be cast in a different light in France, where Americanism implicitly suggested a program of action. The war had been fought entirely on French soil and, in the face of immense damage, the task and the word that hung on everyone's lips was *reconstruction.* While the majority of French artists, architects, writers, and businessmen shied away from innovation, preferring to bask in dreams of reconstructing the French patrimony *à l'dentique,* exactly the way it had looked before the war, a few individuals did engage in the modernist dream of the tabula rasa. This perspective marked the postwar collaboration between the architect and painter Le Corbusier and the painter Amédée Ozenfant. It was most cogently articulated in their two Parisian manifestos: *Après le Cubisme* of 1918 and "Purism," published in the January 1921 issue of their magazine *L'Esprit Nouveau.* In accord with the moralizing climate of the postwar years in France—a climate that was given a name at the time, *le rappel à l'ordre,* or call to order—these texts provided a set of aesthetic correctives to counter the supposed failings of the immediate prewar period. The chaos, illegibility, and deconstructive drive of Cubism were to be replaced by order, clarity, and balance. Bergsonian flux and duration were to give way to a search for constants via a Neoplatonic romance with the realm of perfect solids. Clearly, the entire ideology of Purism was predicated on the repression of the trauma of war.[4] Meanwhile, the strict alignment of streamlined objects, the stereometric projections, and the overlapping of forms in Le Corbusier's and Ozenfant's Purist still lifes (fig. 4) pointed to the practice of architecture and the efficiency of the assembly line. The towering profiles of their bottles, glasses, guitars, and shafts are unmistakably transpositions into tabletop compositions of the photographs of American grain elevators and airplane hangars reproduced in *L'Esprit Nouveau.*

That architecture must learn the lessons of Taylorism and Fordism or perish was Le Corbusier's repeated message.[5] Architecture or revolution? he asked. Only an efficient approach to the former would preclude the social disruption of the latter. Rationalism, standardization, and mass-production remained the leitmotifs of his publications throughout the 1920s and of his repeated *Appels aux industriels* (Calls to Industrialists). Most spectacularly American was his *Contemporary City for Three Million People* (fig. 28), presented as a diorama at the Salon d'Automne in 1922. Properly spaced with greenery, his rows of skyscrapers were conceived as a utopian corrective to what he saw as the mad overcrowding of Manhattan: "Let's listen to American engineers, but let's fear American architects" was one of Le Corbusier's favorite sayings a few years later.[6] Such a distinction is certainly telling. For all too often the French admiration for American innovation went hand in hand with an equal disdain for what was perceived as its cultural dependence on Europe. Thus, while they felt ready to emulate America in terms of its material culture, it was no place, as far as they were concerned, for high culture.

While Le Corbusier and Ozenfant expurged from their own art the heterogeneous clutter of everyday life and mass culture, it filled the pages of *L'Esprit Nouveau* with a layout and hard-selling techniques that competed, ultimately, with those of American magazines. This heterogeneity continued to be an inspiration for an artist like Fernand Léger, who was wary of the excessive rigors of Purism. *The*

28. Le Corbusier. *Contemporary City for Three Million Inhabitants. Perspective Diorama of City Center.* 1922. India ink on tracing paper, 26 x 51⅝". Fondation Le Corbusier, Paris, FLC 31005

City, 1919 (Philadelphia Museum of Art), Léger's most ambitious work of the immediate postwar years, is ordered along the grid. Yet his inclusion of the figure, billboards, and advertisements countered strict regularity with a sense of the disorder of a particular (and most typically American) urban scene.

During the 1920s, the French had several occasions to look at American Precisionism in Paris. *Seven Americans,* a show organized by the Whitney Studio Club in New York, traveled to the Galeries Durand-Ruel in 1923 and included, among more conservative artists, Charles Sheeler and Charles Demuth. A trinational exhibition was held again at Durand-Ruel in 1925 with works by Sheeler, who was also represented at a multinational show at the Galerie Bernheim-Jeune in 1927. But, as several American critics lamented in their reviews of *Seven Americans,* the energy of French critics seemed entirely directed toward source hunting and to what they saw as derivations from French art.[7] Slightly greater attention was paid to Sheeler's photographs than to his paintings. In 1927, *Cahiers d'art* devoted a two-page spread to his New York photographs. In 1929, Eugene Jolas wrote, after Sheeler showed him some of his River Rouge photographs during a trip to Paris that year, "The almost puritanical rigidity of his studies should not blind us to the inner force and beauty inherent in them. The illusions of plane are perfect. There is nothing decorative about them. They are the mechanical-chemical reflections of the imagination."[8] Yet on the whole, while they relished the presence of American expatriates eager to assimilate into French culture by sitting at the Montparnasse cafés—and even in the presence of such true Americans in Paris as authors Ernest Hemingway and F. Scott Fitzgerald—French critics paid precious little attention to artists like Sheeler, Demuth, Patrick Henry Bruce, Niles Spencer, or Stuart Davis, all of whom spent some time in Paris in the twenties.

The exception may have been Gerald Murphy, who received a good deal of attention during his stay in Paris from 1921 to 1924. Murphy had the nerve (as the French would see it) to send a huge canvas to the Salon des Indépendants in 1924, provoking a heated controversy among the Salon's organizers when its size required that it be removed from the American Room (the Salon was hung according to nationalities) to the far more prominent entrance hall of the Grand Palais.[9] Entitled *Boatdeck,* the Purist-influenced painting was, like Sheeler's *Upper Deck* (fig. 10) or Demuth's *Paquebot "Paris"* (fig. 11), about the streamlined vehicles of transatlantic travel. And, of course, the *Paris,* the *Olympic,* the *Europa,* the *Île de France,* the *Lafayette,* the *Normandie,* those fantastic floating cities, the huge Corbusean machines-to-live-in launched by the French and the Americans, symbolized better than any other achievements of the interwar years the passage from one continent to the other, the link between the old and the new continents via the wonders of technology. Yet if his regular Salon submissions from 1922 to 1926 earned Murphy some honorable mentions in French publications, the artist had no feature article and no solo exhibition in Paris until his show at Bernheim-Jeune in 1936.

Another American artist who did manage to achieve a minimal degree of visibility was Louis Lozowick, who, after two years in Paris in 1920–22 and three in Berlin, kept in touch with the editors of *L'Esprit Nouveau* following his return to the United States. In 1928, he had a solo show at Galerie Zak in Paris; in the accompanying catalogue the critic Waldemar George praised his "precise and impeccable craftsmanship" and the way in which "he constructs his American cityscapes like an architect designs a perspective, like an engineer devises a plan."[10]

Equally little attention was paid to those few inveterate America lovers among French artists who followed Duchamp's and Picabia's earlier example in visiting the United States in the 1920s. Bernard Boutet de Monvel's vertiginous bird's-eye views of New York skyscrapers, painted in 1926 and deeply influenced by Sheeler's paintings and photographs (fig. 29), were overlooked. Jacques Mauny's submissions to the 1925 and 1926 Salons, two versions of a painting entitled *New York/Baseball,* initially commanded some attention in his native country, earning him a solo show at the Galerie Druet. Mauny was a go-between for the two continents, sending his Paris letter to *The Arts* and his New York reviews to *L'Art vivant* each time he crossed the Atlantic. In "New York–1926," one of the few articles about contemporary American art published in a French art magazine, he celebrated the work ethic and the accelerated tempo symbolized by the skyscraper, adding: "The American aesthetic is asexual, it prefers intellectual games to sensual ones. Severity, austerity, the pristine air of the North American coast, the precision of Murphy's and Sheeler's paintings, are the expression of the Americans' love for perfection devoid of graceful and superfluous detail."[11]

After a decade of vacillating between enthusiasm for and obliviousness toward America, the French disposition changed substantially in 1927, the year marking the official end of postwar reconstruction. That year, André Tardieu, André Siegfried, and Lucien Romier—a minister in the French government, a renowned university professor, and an economist, respectively—published, again respectively, *Devant l'obstacle; L'Amérique et nous, les États Unis d'aujourd'hui;* and *Qui sera le maître? Europe ou Amérique,* three books that reflected the authors' spectacular about-face adopting a markedly anti-American stance after years of wholesale advocacy of the American system. Forerunners of the wave of anti-Americanism that swept France during the Depression, all three set up a Manichean dichotomy between a healthy, balanced (that is, semiagrarian), human, rooted France and the "total proletarization" and dehumanization of an overurbanized America whose society had abdicated to mass culture, and

29. Bernard Boutet de Monvel. *New York.* Oil on canvas, 41 x 26¾". Private Collection; courtesy Barry Friedman, Ltd.

worse, to what Romier called "mass life." Clearly, much of their criticism and bitterness stemmed from France's inability to maintain its position in the forefront of world affairs in spite of its victory and speedy recovery. Meanwhile, it is no coincidence that these books were published just as Germany had regained its prewar position as the number one economic power in Europe. The resurrection of France's perennial foe was largely the result of America's Dawes Plan of 1924. For its implementation had allowed an enormous infiltration of American credits, manufactured goods, and cultural imports into the German economy and, reciprocally, a considerable reduction of German war reparations owed to France. As a result, the plan not only reinforced Germany but bruised French illusions of being released of its own war debt to England and the United States by the comforting motto *l'Allemagne payera* (Germany will pay).

Significantly then, France's distancing from the United States coincided with Germany's rapprochement with things American. Even more than the French, the Germans had a history of fascination and ambivalence toward America. On the one hand, they celebrated American vitality, all the more so since they had undergone (unlike France) an industrialization and urbanization whose speed and ruthlessness could only be compared to America's. Conversely, one heard countless Spenglerian cries about American influence signaling the decline of the West: cries all the more acute in a country that specifically distinguished between the notion of *Kultur* (spiritual, high culture) and *Zivilisation* (material, debased, antinational modes of living).[12]

Indeed, while the Parisians had virtually no propensity to envisage their city as anything but French, Berlin, with its rambling topography, its chaotic admixture of old and new, and its habit of demolishing anything more than fifty years old, was described as the most American city in Europe.[13] After his move to Berlin in 1924, playwright Bertolt Brecht—and artists close to him like Rudolf Schlichter and Karl Hubbuch—repeatedly satirized Berlin as the "cold Chicago," or as an imaginary boomtown populated by dashing gangsters pursued by cohorts of enemy gangs, in such works as *The Rise and Fall of Mahagonny* of 1930. It was also in 1924 that the Expressionist architect Erich Mendelsohn visited New York, Chicago, Detroit, and Buffalo and returned with a set of photographs that, printed oversize in 1926 as a picture book entitled *Amerika. Bilderbuch eines Architekten* (America: An Architect's Picture Book), enjoyed an extraordinary success among architects, writers (including Brecht), and lay people alike. While some of his photographs were reminiscent of Sheeler's urban industrial photography, Mendelsohn preserved the human factor, the heterogeneity of the city crowds. In his preface, Mendelsohn articulated the typical European's view of America as a distorting mirror of Europe, that is, both as a site of utopia and a warning of things to come.

Similarly, it was during a trip to New York in 1924 that Fritz Lang conceived of his film *Metropolis*, released three years later. An attack on the enslavement of the worker in the factory, it was also one of the most spectacular, seductive cinematic renderings of mythologized and feminized technology-out-of-control ever conceived.

Meanwhile, the enthusiastic reception of the German edition of Henry Ford's biography in 1923 had already indicated that a large number of Germans (in contrast to a minority in France) recognized in Scientific Management the way out of the economic chaos of the early Weimar years. It should be no surprise, then, that in 1923, three years before its move from Weimar to Gropius's landmark metal and glass building in Dessau, the Bauhaus abandoned Expressionism, arts and crafts, and other medievalizing utopias in favor of the *Realpolitik* of the machine age. Under the influence of the charismatic Moholy-Nagy, who was appointed by Gropius in 1923 to a key position at the school, and allied under Gropius's own motto "Art and Technology, a New Unity," its paradigms shifted: the *Bauhütte* (or phalanstery) became a factory, and the workshops became laboratories. Indeed Gropius, even earlier than Le Corbusier, had praised the monumentality of American industrial architecture as comparable to the realizations of the ancient Egyptians.[14] But it was only with the move to industrial Dessau in 1926, and the financial backing of Junkers, the aeronautic industry based in that city, that art and design were de facto wed to industry. German interest in contemporary American art and urban industrial society was also evidenced that year by a feature article in *Das Kunstblatt* that hailed Sheeler as the prime "master of exactitude" and reproduced his *MacDougal Alley* (plate 12).[15]

Although Moholy-Nagy and Sheeler entertained a far more ambivalent view of technology than did the advocates of the Bauhaus, or most of the American Precisionists, the technical precision that characterized their work was also the dominant trait of the paintings exhibited in *"Neue Sachlichkeit": Deutsche Malerei seit dem Expressionismus* ("New Objectivity": German Painting Since Expressionism) at the Stadt Kunsthalle in Mannheim in 1925. German in scope (although it included Lozowick), the show included a wide variety of works.[16] Yet whether the paintings belonged to what G. F. Hartlaub referred to in his exhibition catalogue as the left-wing "verism" charac-

30. Carl Grossberg. *The Yellow Kettle*. 1933. Oil on wood, 36 x 28". Von der Heydt-Wuppertal Museum, Germany

teristic of Berlin art (for example, that of George Grosz, Karl Hubbuch, and Otto Dix), or to the more conservative, "classical," *Neue Biedermeier* trend characteristic of smaller cities like Munich, Kallel, and Karlsruhe, where, respectively, Carlo Mense, Kay H. Nebel, or Wilhelm Schnarenberger were based, these artists all shared a "*wille sur sachlichkeit*," a drive toward the factual, the cold, the objective, an emphasis on what we may translate as the depiction of "thingness," and a highly technical attention to detail. That year, art critic Franz Roh enlarged the definition of *sachlich* art to include paintings by a significant number of Italian, French, and American artists (among the latter, Lozowick and Axel Nilzon) in his book *Nach-Expressionismus–Magischer Realismus: Probleme der Neuesten Europaischen Malerei* (Post Expressionism–Magic Realism: Problems of the Most Recent European Painting). Roh's concept of magic realism, referring to the pervasive influence of Giorgio de Chirico's metaphysical paintings, was very perceptive. It underscored the ultimate eeriness of those images that claimed to capture, during the 1920s, the so-called objectivity of the modern spirit. It also dramatized by extension, on a quasi philosophical level, the impossibility to grasp the real. The term caught on and a few years later Jolas spoke of magic realism in his aforementioned discussion of Sheeler's work. Most intriguing in this respect are the paintings of an artist like Karl Grossberg, who, after a brief stint at the Bauhaus in 1921, spent the rest of his life in isolation in an old tower in the rural town of Sommerhausen near Würzburg. While his machines, trapped in insulation rooms in the company of a lone bat or monkey (fig. 30), owed much to de Chirico, his depictions of empty industrial neighborhoods, oil tanks, and loading docks accentuated the eeriness that permeated the paintings of Demuth and Sheeler.

It is in photography, however, that the technical precision, emotional detachment, sobriety, and impersonality of the *sachlich* spirit found its medium. Opposed to the fanciful croppings and the experimental approach of Bauhaus photographers like Moholy-Nagy, Albert Renger-Patzsch capitalized on the glacial, razor-sharp focus afforded by new camera lenses. In his photo book *Die Welt ist schön* (The World Is Beautiful) of 1928, beauty is synonymous with geometry and seriality. Omitting landscapes and humans as too romantic and too pictorialist, Renger-Patzsch's beautiful world is one of close-ups of flowers, factories, and objects aligned on a conveyor belt juxtaposed without a word of commentary: structure speaks. Another photographer, Werner Mantz, restricted himself to architecture (fig. 31), zeroing in on the standardized, mass-produced aesthetic championed by Gropius, Bruno Taut, Martin Wagner, and Hugo Haring in projects like the workers housing blocks of Berlin-Britz and Berlin-Siemensstadt, built on the southeastern edge of the city. Unique in Europe at the time, these projects had their epigones in virtually every middle-sized city in Germany by the late 1920s.

There was, for sure, a shared sensibility between the work of German *sachlich* photography and that of the Americans—Edward Weston, Imogen Cunningham, Paul Outerbridge, and Sheeler—all of whom were included in the important *Film und Foto* exhibition in Stuttgart in 1929. The show featured more than a thousand works by photographers and filmmakers from Western Europe, the Soviet Union, and the United States. Not only was Weston asked to select works by American photographers for the exhibition, but he also wrote the foreword to the American section of the catalogue. Contemporary reviews especially praised American contributions; Carl Georg Heise, one of the most important writers on photography, singled out a Weston photograph as "one of the peak productions of the whole exhibition."[17]

Interestingly, *sachlich* photography had no real counterpart in France. There, the work of André Kertész, Man Ray, and Brassaï remained under the spell of Surrealism and subjective to the extreme. The only exception, derived from their German experience, was the photography of Germaine Krull and Florence Henri: bodies of work all the more exceptional in the context of an overwhelmingly male aesthetic. Krull spent years in Munich, where she set up her own portrait studio, then she was in Berlin and Holland. In 1927, her most important book, *Metal,* was published in Paris. Based on shots of industrial machines, swooping perspectives, and close-ups of steel constructions in latticed iron, such as the Eiffel Tower and the Rotterdam Transporter Bridge, Krull's vision had a greater affinity with Moholy-Nagy's than Renger-Patzsch's.

Florence Henri's life followed a trajectory that is directly in line with the themes of this essay. Born in New York of a French father and a German mother, she studied first in Paris with Léger and Ozenfant in the early twenties, then with Moholy and Albers at the Bauhaus in Dessau. In 1929, she returned to Paris. As a result of her training, while the dramatic black on white contrasts of her studio work captured the stylized elegance of Purist still lifes, the sharp camera-angles and surprising geometric patterns of her urban photographs remained, after her return to Paris, very much in keeping with the Bauhaus aesthetic.

With the onset of the Great Depression, the course of modernity and, by consequence, that of Americanism, was irrevocably altered. By 1930, three years before the Nazi takeover, a number of German modernist artists, architects, photographers, and critics had grown disillusioned with the anonymity of the *sachlich* style. Shaken by the stock market crash and capitalism's attendant convulsions, they sought to recover the lost *aura* of the work of art, in the famous words of Walter Benjamin, in the process of industrialization.[18] Vasily Kandinsky continued to teach until the Bauhaus was shut down by the Nazis in 1933, but in 1930, Paul Klee and Oskar Schlemmer resigned, discouraged by the increasingly Productivist and anti-painting turn taken by the school. Similarly, less than a year after *Film und Foto,* Werkbund member Paul Renner gave a pessimistic account of the tyranny of an all-pervading machine civilization in his opening address at the Munich exhibition *Das Lichtbild* (The Photograph) in 1930. In addition, as several socialist architects like Bruno Taut and Hannes Meyer left Germany, after subsidies dried up in 1929, to work in the Soviet Union, *sachlich* architecture came increasingly under attack in the popular and the right-wing press for its

31. Werner Mantz. *Entrance, Residential Apartment Block, Kalkerfeld, Cologne.* 1928. Gelatin silver print, 15⅛ x 8¾". The Metropolitan Museum of Art, New York. Ford Motor Company Collection, Gift of Ford Motor Company and John C. Waddell, 1987.1100.30

deadly uniformity and the coldness of its naked facades.[19] Meanwhile, it was, ironically enough, during the Depression that Léger and Le Corbusier, the two great champions of the machine aesthetic in France, finally made their visits to America—Léger in 1931, with Le Corbusier on board the newly built *Normandie* in 1935, and alone again in 1938.

Ultimately, these trips, which have long been viewed by art historians as yet another chapter in the saga of high modernism, were ideologically critical ones. By the time of their visit to the United States, the work of both Léger and Le Corbusier had undergone a fundamental change. In a France torn between myriad plans aimed at solving the Depression, it had shifted from a total dedication to the rectilinear geometries and efficiency of the machine to organicism and the neoconservative creeds of regionalism and corporatism—thus paralleling tendencies in American society and art.[20] In "New York vu par Fernand Léger," published in 1931 upon his return from his first trip, the painter spoke of his elation in front of the most colossal spectacle in the world. But, he added, "Mechanical life is here at its apogee. It has reached the ceiling, overshot the mark . . . crisis! American life is a succession of adventures optimistically pushed as far as they will go. They have risked everything, tried everything. . . . Naturally, if I stop and start thinking, if I close my eyes, I sense all the tragedies that lurk around this exaggerated dynamism, but I came to look and so I go on looking."[21]

And so the Europeans kept on looking, with a mixture of anxiety and self-vindication, at America as the epicenter of the Depression. Yet by the time European artists and intellectuals began to arrive en masse in the United States—coming now not to experience the ultimate in modernity, but to flee Nazi persecution, World War II, and, after 1940, the collaborationist regime of Vichy—the history of American Precisionism was essentially over.

NOTES

1. "French Artists Spur On an American Art," *The New York Tribune*, October 24, 1915, p. 2.

2. See Rudolf Kuenzli, ed., *New York Dada* (New York: Willis Locker and Owens, 1986), pp. 52–65.

3. Quoted in William A. Camfield, "Marcel Duchamp's Fountain: Its History and Aesthetics in the Context of 1917," *Dada/Surrealism*, no. 16, 1987, pp. 64–94.

4. I am indebted to Kenneth Silver's *Esprit de Corps: The Art of the Parisian Avant-Garde and the First World War, 1915–1925* (Princeton: Princeton University Press, 1989).

5. See Mary McLeod, "Architecture or Revolution: Taylorism, Technocracy, and Social Change," *Art Journal*, Summer 1983, pp. 132–47.

6. Quoted in Mardges Bacon, *Américanisme et modernité: L'idéal américain dans l'architecture* (Paris: Flammarion, 1993), p. 193.

7. "Some French Critics Voice Opinion on American Art," *Evening Post*, February 2, 1924, and other clippings, H.E. Schankenberg Papers, Archives of American Art, Smithsonian Institution, roll 851, frame 915. See also Elisabeth Hutton Turner, *American Artists in Paris 1919–1929* (Ann Arbor and London: UMI Research Press, 1989), pp. 60–62.

8. See "Photographies de New York par Charles Sheeler," *Cahiers d'art*, no. [illegible], [illegible], pp. 130–32; and Eugene Jolas, "The Industrial Mythos," *Transition* (Paris and New York), no. 18, November 1929, pp. 123–29.

9. "American's Eighteen Foot Picture Nearly Splits Independants Artists," *The New York Herald* (Paris), February 8, 1924, pp. 1–2.

10. Waldemar George, "Paysages d'Amérique," *Exp. de dessins et gravures de LL*, exh. cat. (Galerie Zak, Paris, 1928), unpaginated.

11. Jacques Mauny, "New York–1926," *L'Art vivant*, January 15, 1926, pp. 53–60. Among the illustrated works were Preston Dickinson's *Industry* (plate 50) and Sheeler's *New York* (plate 8).

12. See *Envisioning America: Prints, Drawings and Photographs by George Grosz and His Contemporaries, 1915–1933*, exh. cat. (Cambridge, Massachusetts: Bush-Reisinger Museum, 1990).

13. See Ian Boyd Whyte, "Berlin 1870–1945: An Introduction Framed by Architecture," in *The Divided Heritage: Themes and Problems in German Modernism*, Irit Rogoff, ed. (Cambridge, Massachusetts: Cambridge University Press, 1991), pp. 223–52.

14. Reyner Banham, *A Concrete Atlantis: U.S. Industrial Building and European Modern Architecture, 1900–1925* (Cambridge, Massachusetts, and London: The MIT Press, 1986), pp. 6, 9, 15, 22. In addition, Moholy-Nagy included one of Sheeler's River Rouge photographs in his Bauhaus book of 1929, *Von Materiel zu Architektur.*

15. See Ruth Green Harris, "Die Neue Malerei in Amerika," *Das Kunstblatt*, November 1926, p. 421. She also discusses the work of George Ault, Demuth, and Alfred Stieglitz.

16. See Patrick Leonard Stewart, "Charles Sheeler, William Carlos Williams, and the Development of the Precisionist Aesthetic," Ph.D. diss., University of Delaware, 1981, p. 131. Bruno W. Reimann, "Louis Lozowick," *Jahrbuch der Junge Kunst* (1923) refers to Lozowick's exemplary precision and calls *Cleveland* (plate 15) a document of the highest *sachlichkeit* (pp. 312–15).

17. Quoted in David Mellor, ed., *Germany: The New Photography, 1927–33* (London: Arts Council of Great Britain, 1978), p. 81.

18. See Walter Benjamin, "The Work of Art at the Age of Mechanical Reproduction" (1936), reprinted in Hannah Arendt, ed., *Illuminations* (New York: Schocken Books, 1968).

19. See Whyte in *The Divided Heritage*, pp. 240–42.

20. See Romy Golan, "A Moralized Landscape: French Art and Ideology Between the Two World Wars," Ph.D. diss., The Courtauld Institute of Art, London, 1989.

21. Fernand Léger, "New York vu par Fernand Léger," *Cahiers d'art*, no. 9, 1931, pp. 84–85, reprinted in *Functions of Painting by Fernand Léger*, Edward F. Fry, ed. (New York: Viking Press, Inc., 1973), pp. 84–85.

THE PRECISIONISTS AND THE POETS

Lisa M. Steinman

WRITERS AND ARTISTS INVOLVED in various avant-garde movements in the United States between 1909 and the 1930s felt they were involved in a common venture; they mutually influenced one another and were in turn influenced by the material culture of early twentieth-century America as well as by anxieties about the place of the arts in that culture. This was a period of manifestos and self-conscious movements, but there were also less-defined interactions, including those involving the visual artists we now call the Precisionists, a number of whom were associated with Alfred Stieglitz.

Concerns about (as William Carlos Williams wrote in 1914) how to "be a mirror to . . . modernity"[1] were further shaped by Stieglitz's and others' introduction of European art movements to the United States early in the century. Stieglitz's special number of *Camera Work* in 1912, for instance, included reproductions of French modern art, as well as two prose pieces on Picasso and Matisse by Gertrude Stein in which, Stieglitz announced, "the Post-Impressionist spirit is found expressing itself in literary form." Thus, he identified Stein's work as not just about but participating in a modern "attitude," which he did not limit to painting or sculpture.[2] Many American writers expressed a similar sense that something new was in the air and that this new spirit, while intimately connected with developments in the visual arts, was not limited to any one art form. Williams, again, looking back at what prompted his early poetic experiments, asked: "What were we seeking? No one knew consistently enough to formulate 'a movement.' We were . . . closely allied with the painters. . . . We had followed [Ezra] Pound's instructions."[3] As Williams's statement suggests, the modernist impulse in American writing was not a formal movement with an attendant manifesto; the sense of a common language and shared venture was in part a result of interpersonal relations, as Williams reveals in titling one chapter in his *Autobiography* "Painters and Parties."

Williams had made friends with the painter Charles Demuth by 1903–4, when they were both students in Philadelphia;[4] by 1923, he had become friends with the photographer and painter Charles Sheeler. Marianne Moore, Wallace Stevens, and Mina Loy moved in the same or overlapping art circles, and their ideas, like Williams's, were informed by exchanges that took place not only in public forums such as magazines and shows, but also at the literary and art salons found between 1909 and 1929 in places like Stieglitz's 291, the apartment of Louise and Walter Arensberg in New York, or Alfred Kreymborg's house in Grantwood, New Jersey. Many people were, to use Williams's word, "allied" simply because they gathered in the same places.[5] Stieglitz and 291 provided the earliest gathering place. Moore while a senior in college at Bryn Mawr, in 1909, jotted in her notebook Stieglitz's name and the address 291 Fifth Avenue; she also wrote to Pound that there was "more evidence of power among painters and sculptors than among writers" in America, indicating that the art scene made New York *the* place to be, even for writers.[6] Marsden Hartley's tribute to Stieglitz conveys the excitement felt by people visiting 291: "A morning in this room with the [central] brass bowl [on green burlap] was revealing, for a smart array of stylish personages appeared and stood about, for there was no place to sit except on the edges of the brass bowl and few there were who felt courage enough to disturb this very awesome symbol."[7]

Moore's 1923 poem "Bowls" seems to be about the game played on a bowling green ("on the green / with lignum vitae balls and ivory markers, / the pins planted in wild duck formation, / and quickly dispersed").[8] But given Moore's admiration for the Precisionists, her usual method of literary collage, and the subject of such contemporaneous poems as "New York" and "People's Surroundings," one suspects Stieglitz's brass bowl on green burlap, perhaps conflated with Paul Strand's *Abstraction-Bowls, 1915,* informs Moore's poem.[9] In "Bowls," the pins "quickly dispersed," like ducks in transit, become emblems of Moore's style in the poem, where images are presented in precise and vivid detail, but quickly replaced. "Bowls" goes on to images of Pompeii, of etymology, of magazine publication, and of letter writing, all of which juxtapose permanence with ephemera, a juxtaposition captured etymologically in "lignum vitae," or the wood of life, a substance, like language itself, that is hard yet also in the process of growth. Further, Moore's style—precise, juxtaposed images that suggest and describe motion—is one that might easily describe some of the American art she admired, such as Demuth's.

Moore seems to have included herself among the practitioners of the new when she wrote in "Bowls," "I learn that we are precisionists, / not citizens of Pompeii arrested in action."[10] Moore's verbal equivalent of a visual style helps suggest how rich and complex the exchanges between Precisionist artists and poets were; that is, while an important part of the exchange involved people who wanted to be part of a vaguely defined new, modern movement, and who like Moore found or located themselves in the places associated with this movement, a further alchemy took place as the vocabulary of one art was translated into another and as European developments were transmuted in the rather different cultural context of early twentieth-century America. This play between visual and verbal elements then influenced not only American painters like Demuth but also writers like Williams.

Williams associated his work with Pound's as well as with the painters'. In 1913, the year of the Armory Show, Pound published his Imagist manifesto, in which he advised writers to use "no superfluous word, no adjective which does not reveal something . . . either no ornament or good ornament" and to go "in fear of abstractions."[11] His injunction—to write a spare, unornamented prose, without verbal abstractions (Pound's example is "dim lands *of peace*")—was then associated with the clean lines of a machine style, and the references to urban, industrial, or commercial culture found in the visual arts. In Spring 1923, the French painter Fernand Léger dedicated an influential essay, "The Esthetics of the Machine," to Pound. But despite assumptions like Léger's and Williams's that Pound defined a machine aesthetic for writers, the literary equivalent of "clean lines" was not obvious. Pound's call for no abstractions or superfluous words defined stylistic features that might well be called clean, but there was also an unconscious pun involved in equating the "clean lines" of hygienic technology with those of artists, let alone with short lines and the avoidance of adjectives. Leo Stein, in fact, protested at the time that "accuracy could hardly be more utterly in default than in a *precise* application of the word 'accurate' to literature" (emphasis added).[12] Nonetheless, Williams, for instance, clearly associated his poems with the taste Léger and Marcel Duchamp promoted as related to American industrial products. In 1921, Williams argued that "American plumbing [and] American bridges" were "notable" because of a national talent for "paying naked attention first to the thing itself," concluding "we are timid in believing that in the arts discovery and invention will take the same course" as technological innovation.[13] What Williams meant when he associated his poems with a machine aesthetic varied, however. He is best known for his minimalist use of language in early poems like "The Red Wheelbarrow" or "Young Sycamore." These poems consist of terse descriptions of a single scene, one way in which Williams embodies the idea of "naked attention to the thing itself," which he associated with American technological production and with Pound's injunctions to stay with "the concrete": "the natural object is always the *adequate* symbol."[14] As in his reference to plumbing and bridges, or in his description for Sheeler's 1939 Museum of Modern Art show in which he echoes Dewey on how "the local is the universal," "the thing itself" appears to be the object represented in paintings and poems, with an emphasis on indigenous objects like Shaker furniture.[15]

Yet elsewhere, comparing Cubist painting with poems, he sounded more like Stein when he emphasized the *poem* as an object; as he wrote in 1923, works of art "must be real, not 'realism' but reality itself. . . . It is not a matter of 'representation.' "[16] At other times, he identified the literary analogue of modern art as having to do primarily with style: "the poetic line, the way the image . . . [lies] on the page."[17] Most often, Williams's interpretation of things or the local took into account Dewey's caution that for writers locality was not a matter of setting or local color but of lives and actions.[18]

In the same way he struggled in his prose to clarify his ideas about how poems might be—or be like or be about—American things, Williams's poems embody various poetic strategies. For him, in fact, it is often unclear whether style or content marks his experiments with a modern American style. As early as 1916, Williams was writing poems like "Pastoral," which begins:

When I was younger
It was plain to me
I must make something of myself.
Older now
I walk back streets
admiring the houses
of the very poor:
roof out of line with sides
the yards cluttered
with old chicken wire, ashes. . . .[19]

The poem can be seen as informed by the Cubist lines and machine aesthetic of Francis Picabia or Léger, as reinterpreted in an American context by Stieglitz or Strand. (Strand's first show at 291 and his piece *Abstraction, Porch Shadows, Twin Lakes, Connecticut* date from the same year as Williams's poem.) Like the Precisionists, Williams uses an American subject matter (including the attitude that one must make something of oneself in the sense of getting ahead with business, as an American male). Debates about localism and American civilization help account for the edgy way in which "Pastoral" positions cultural attitudes about what is important (making something of oneself) against its appreciation of a certain aesthetic. The poem goes on to note that the scenes of urban decay, when tinted a certain bluish-green, "please [the speaker] best" and ends, "No one / will believe this / of vast import to the nation." The use of "import" balances the import-export economic values of the United States against the aesthetic and poetic vision Williams celebrates. At the same time, the very way the words are arranged on the page allies the poem with a machine aesthetic. The lines are determined not by meter or rhyme, but by the length of the typewritten words, forming a visual as well as a verbal text.[20]

Stevens, another poet who frequented places like the Arensbergs' salon, noted "it would be possible to study poetry by studying painting," although he added that just "as poets can be affected by the *sayings* of painters, so can painters be affected by the *sayings* of poets" (emphasis added).[21] Stevens's careful phrasing underlines the role rhetoric about the arts played in the interactions between the visual and the literary arts. Even Williams's attention to his poems as visual objects came not only from looking at art but from statements like Stieglitz's on the pieces exhibited in the 1917 Independents Exhibition: "each bit of work [should] stand on its own merits. As a reality. The public would be purchasing its own reality and not a commercialized and inflated name. . . . The independence of the work itself."[22]

In their awareness of an American context, and association of "clean lines" with America, Williams's and Moore's poetry and poetics recall Sheeler's accurate representations of American scenes. But in their emphasis on creative process, the writers eschew the literary equivalent of Sheeler's realism; the "things" in their poems—outhouses and city trees—are presented in a style that almost never maintains a seamless, realistic description or narrative, but that calls attention to voice (as in Williams's "Young Sycamore") or rapidly replaces one image by another (as in Moore's "Bowls").

Henry Sayre has proposed that Sheeler's late description of *Upper Deck* (fig. 10) might stand as the best description of American Precisionism in the arts:

32. Charles Demuth. *I Saw the Figure 5 in Gold.* 1928. Oil on board, 35½ x 30". The Metropolitan Museum of Art, New York. Alfred Stieglitz Collection, 49.59.1

"I had come to feel that a picture could have incorporated in it the structural design implied in abstraction and be presented in a wholly realistic manner."[23] Sheeler thus distinguishes his use of realism from the more abstract compositions of European artists. Strand further identified the difference (and, tacitly, the desire to insist on a difference) between American and European modernism, writing that American "photographers learned from the abstract painters, but we did not follow them except momentarily into the purely abstract. We went on exploring America."[24] As with the writers, such statements by these artists stem in part from a defensiveness about the arts in America and, again, what it meant to explore America varied widely in practice.

Although most were aware of debates about American culture, not all of the Precisionists followed Strand and Sheeler in their insistence that the way to underline the "American-ness" of a machine aesthetic was by maintaining both geometric forms and realistic representations of American subject matter. The same issue of *The Blind Man* containing Stieglitz's letter about the reality of the art object in itself contained a poem by Charles Demuth, which ends:

> *So many say that they say*
> *nothing,—but these never really send.*
> *For some there is no stopping*
> *Most stop or get a style.*
> *When they stop they make*
> *a convention*
> *That is their end.*
> *For the going every thing*
> *has an idea.*
> *The going run right along.*
> *The going just keep going.*[25]

Demuth's poem is derivative of Stein with its use of repetition and its play on verb forms ("noth*ing*" "stopp*ing*" "go*ing*" "th*ing*"); like Stein also, as well as like Moore who disclaims those "arrested in action," Demuth emphasizes movement—the "going just keep going"—even as he transmutes a colloquial platitude ("When the going gets tough, the tough get going"). Similarly, Demuth's portrait posters, from the 1920s, although they are in the tradition of Picabia's object portraits, retranslate the genre through literary models, not only Stein's but also, by the twenties, Williams's.[26]

Demuth's best-known poster, in fact, is his 1928 portrait of Williams, *I Saw the Figure 5 in Gold* (fig. 32), whose title he took from Williams's poem "The Great Figure":

> *Among the rain*
> *and lights*
> *I saw the figure 5*
> *in gold*
> *on a red*
> *firetruck*
> *moving. . . .*[27]

As Wanda Corn has noted, Demuth's portrait-posters are full of double entendres, including various linguistic turns, as with the words "[T]Art Co." that appear in *I Saw the Figure 5 in Gold*. Corn also points out how, in Demuth's painting, "the visual field is more energetic and unstable than the taut picture drawn by [Williams's] poem . . . Demuth's . . . compositional lines and receding 5's forcing the eye to zoom in and out of the painting in constant movement. But perhaps the most important difference between the poem and the painting is the prominent role Demuth assigned to language. While the poem never takes us on side trips, the painting teases us away from the main event with partial words, letters, and numbers that beg to be read and deciphered."[28] Corn's reading of Demuth's painting is compelling; what it helps emphasize also, however, is, first, that paintings and poems may work differently—in particular, motion may be signaled differently on the page and on the canvas; second, what counts as motion—as the painters and poets read one another—may once again be the product of a series of dynamic exchanges that are not easily generalized, especially as one moves from art to literature.

Williams, for instance, seems to have thought of his use of the machine aesthetic at least partially in terms of motion; the lines may be sparse, but they move the eye down the page quickly. They also take the reader on "side trips" by insisting on themselves as visual objects. Williams, in fact, consistently stressed the "*flux* of the seeing eye" and his poems as "notes jotted down in the midst of the *action*" (emphases added).[29] The main verb in "The Great Figure" is "saw," and only on line six does it become clear that the mix of position, color, and figure are seen on a firetruck. Moore, similarly, defended form in modern art and writing as "a corollary to momentum,"[30] a gesture reminiscent of her definition of "precisionists" in "Bowls."

The poets often read even the images of Stieglitz and Strand as involving motion. In some cases, such an assessment of Precisionism in the arts may involve (creative) misunderstanding by writers; yet as early as 1934 a series of tributes to Stieglitz yielded such disparate statements as Williams's on how what Stieglitz's images offer American culture, "isn't a thing: it's an act. If it stands still, it is dead," and Jean Toomer's description of Stieglitz as a "genius of what is . . . this is why he uses a camera, and this is why he will never use a *moving*-picture camera."[31]

Similarly, Strand's description of "crystallization," or capturing a "moment" when forces become "physical and objective," suggests he saw his own work as involving stillness over motion.[32] Yet reviewing the 1925 *Seven Americans* exhibition, Moore wrote of Strand's work: "We welcome the power-house in the drawing-room when we examine his orientally perfect combining of discs, parabolas, and verticals— . . . the depth of tone upon the anaconda-like curves of central bearings."[33] Typically, Moore's language emphasizes the motion of Strand's working (his "combining") as well as adding life to his subject matter ("anaconda-like curves"). In short, whatever Strand intended by pieces like *Akeley Motion Picture Camera, New York* (plate 46), Moore understood his work as indicating motion, a gesture informed again by cultural debates, and especially the commonplace association between America, speed, and activity, an association like that between America and industrial design, which many writers and artists transvalued and claimed.

The writings of many associated with Precisionism—like Moore, Stevens, Demuth, and Williams—betray finally an ambivalent relationship to American culture. Williams's "At the Faucet of June," for instance, invokes an industrial landscape but also comments on the culture of the United States with a portrait of "J. P[ierpont] M[organ]" as a modern version of Pluto, god of wealth, abducting Persephone (or spring, Williams's figure for creativity), in a failed attempt "to solve the core" (a play on Kore, the Greek Persephone):

of whirling flywheels
by cutting

the Gordian knot
with a Veronese or
perhaps a Rubens—[34]

Morgan's art collection, consuming art objects rather than supporting live artists, is implicitly criticized. The poem opens with sunlight "full of a song / inflated to / fifty pounds pressure," which both associates the song with industrial products, like automobile tires, and echoes Stieglitz's caution on mistaking "commercialized and inflated" names for the reality art offers. Yet Williams, while criticizing industrial culture and industrialists, borrows an aesthetic and a subject from the contemporary industrial world.

Perhaps the most cogent comment on the ambivalence found in many of the writers and artists comes from Demuth, who wrote that "America doesn't really care," adding "still, if one is really an artist and at the same time an American, just this not caring . . . can be artistic material."[35] Demuth's "[ ] Art Co.," like Williams's "Pastoral" and "At the Faucet of June," marks, and makes art out of, an uneasiness about a culture that provided material for, yet did not support, the arts. Williams, like Demuth and Moore, was capable of making art of his ambivalence about the cultural icons he claimed. This, in part, informs his quarrel by the thirties with Sheeler, one artist whose work shows no ambivalence about the culture from which it drew.

Williams was briefly associated with the objectivist movement, which related poetry to Sheeler's photographic aesthetic; the objectivist manifesto told readers it was "absolutely necessary" to read Moore, Williams, Stevens, and Pound, and began with a definition taken from optics: "The lens bringing the rays from an object to a focus."[36] But Williams, who was deeply ambivalent about the culture to which such an aesthetic paid homage, did not associate himself with objectivism for long; similarly, by 1938, he voiced the opinion that Sheeler's work was too "impersonal . . . too much [a] withdrawal from life," adding that he "wanted more of a comment . . . [and that] someone should smash [Sheeler's] camera and open his brain."[37] Williams's judgment seems related to his sense that Sheeler, who worked for Condé Nast and—through the N.W. Ayer and Son advertising agency—for Ford, did not have sufficient suspicions of commercial and industrial America. Williams, on the other hand, increasingly called attention to the socioeconomic world glossed over by a machine aesthetic.

The exchange is an active one, which is to say that Sheeler was well aware of what his work omitted: "We are all confronted with social comment, but for myself I am keeping clear of all that. I am interested in intrinsic qualities in art. . . . I don't believe I could ever indulge in social comment."[38] Sheeler's photographs of Ford's Rouge River plant are a case in point. They present an industrial landscape as a version of pastoral, much as Williams's "Pastoral" does with an urban landscape. Sheeler's crispness of image, geometric lines, and suppression of human presence call attention to the beauty of the landscape's planes and lines. Similarly, in his 1931 painting of Ford's plant, *Classic Landscape* (plate 65), the column forms, reduced palette, and title all aestheticize the plant for the viewer. Williams's 1937 poem "Classic Scene" articulates the poet's uneasiness about Sheeler's use of (and Williams's own experiments with) a Precisionist aesthetic.[39] Williams's poem describes and domesticates a powerhouse with "the shape of / a red brick chair / . . . on the seat of which / sit the figures / of two metal / stacks." The seventeen-line poem then ends with objective description. But there is one adjective that stands out as having little to do with description or domestication; the stacks command "an area / of *squalid* shacks" (emphasis added); with one word, Williams adds the social comment Sheeler refuses, suggesting a social "scene," not just a "landscape," although the poem still invokes and, in the very way it sits on the page, celebrates Sheeler's aesthetic. Indeed, that Williams's poem grows out of his disagreement with Sheeler still suggests the close ties between the two. Finally, in the same way that Moore and Williams reread the visual images of Stieglitz and Strand as involving action, so Williams later recast his relationship with Sheeler by misreading *Classic Landscape*.[40] While Sheeler clearly denied any interest in social commentary, by 1954 Williams wrote, "It is hard to believe that a picture such as *Classic Landscape* . . . owes its effectiveness to an arrangement of cylinders and planes in the distance" rather than to the artist's recognition of "man's pitiful weakness and . . . fate in the world."[41] In short, in 1937, Williams's poem argued with Sheeler; by 1954, Williams simply reread Sheeler's art as if it contained the social commentary, the absence of which had bothered Williams earlier.

There is then something far more complicated than the word "influence" usually suggests that marks the interaction of the writers and artists we associate with Precisionism. There was a heady brew—a process—that involved the pure excitement of being part of a new modern movement; the often defensive attempt to define a distinctively American style in the face of Europeans excited about the country's commercial and industrial products while also facing an American public that valued commerce over the arts, especially modern art; and the sometimes uneasy, often idiosyncratic, translation into practice of a rhetoric from a variety of literary, artistic, and political sources. One might take heed, then, of Stevens's comment on defining what he found alive in the arts; there was a strong relationship between American Precisionism in the arts and American modernist poetry, but to "fix it is to put an end to it. [It can only be shown] unfixed."[42]

NOTES

1. A. Walton Litz and Christopher MacGowan, eds., *The Collected Poems of William Carlos Williams, Volume I, 1909–1939* (New York: New Directions, 1986), p. 28.
2. Reprinted in Jacqueline Vaught Brogan, *Part of the Climate: American Cubist Poetry* (Berkeley: University of California Press, 1991), p. 286.
3. *The Autobiography of William Carlos Williams* (New York: Random House, 1951), p. 148.
4. Ibid., p. 52.
5. Williams and Moore wrote about a number of modern artists, including Sheeler, John Marin, Marsden Hartley, and Paul Strand, who were part of Stieglitz's circle. See William Carlos Williams, *The Selected Letters of William Carlos Williams*, John C. Thirlwall, ed. (New York: New Directions, 1957), p. 166; Rick Stewart, "Charles Sheeler, William Carlos Williams, and Precisionism: A Redefinition," *Arts Magazine*, vol. 58, November 1983, p. 105; Mike Weaver, *William Carlos Williams: The American Background* (1971; reprint, Cambridge: Cambridge University Press, 1977), p. 55.
6. January 9, 1919, letter to Ezra Pound, reprinted in Charles Tomlinson, ed., *Marianne Moore: A Collection of Critical Essays* (Englewood Cliffs, New Jersey: Prentice-Hall Inc., 1969), p. 18. Although Moore did not get to see 291 until 1915, her earliest scrapbooks and reading diaries are full of clippings and quotations on the arts, and especially those involving responses to the 1913 Armory Show from journals like *Letters and Arts* and *Current Opinion*.
7. Waldo Frank, Lewis Mumford, Dorothy Norman, Paul Rosenfeld, and Harold Rugg, eds., *America and Alfred Stieglitz: A Collective Portrait* (New York: The Literary Guild, 1934), pp. 237–38.
8. Marianne Moore, *The Complete Poems of Marianne Moore* (New York: Macmillan, 1967), p. 59.
9. Moore admired the art of Hartley, Strand, Sheeler, Demuth, John Marin, and Georgia O'Keeffe. As Charles Molesworth notes in *Marianne Moore: A Literary Life* (New York: Atheneum, 1990), pp. 191, 325, she also met many of the artists through the New York salons and galleries, and in 1923 accompanied Williams on a visit to Demuth.
10. Moore revised "Bowls," which first appeared in *Secession*, vol. 5, July 1923, p. 12, and was reprinted in the 1924 *Observations* and the 1935 *Selected Poems*, for her 1951 *Collected Poems*, where she replaced the original "precisians" with "precisionists," and so retrospectively confirmed her claimed alliance with the artists who had come to be known as Precisionists. In both versions Moore sends her readers to an etymological dictionary to find the root of her work in the Latin *praecidere*, "cut short" or "abridged," again relating to the modernist emphasis (through Pound and the painters) on economy of expression.
11. "A Few Don't's," *Poetry*, vol. 1, March 1913; reprinted in *Literary Essays of Ezra Pound* (Norfolk, Connecticut: New Directions, 1954), pp. 4–5.
12. "Tradition and Art," *Arts*, May 1925, p. 269; the article is cited in Moore's notebooks.
13. "Yours, O Youth," *Contact*, vol. 3, 1921; reprinted in *Selected Essays* (New York: New Directions, 1969), p. 35. Williams read Duchamp's 1917 statement in *The Blind Man* regarding American plumbing and bridges.
14. *Literary Essays of Ezra Pound*, p. 5.
15. See *Charles Sheeler: paintings drawings photographs* (New York: The Museum of Modern Art, 1939), pp. 7–8, and John Dewey, "Americanism and Localism," *Dial*, vol. 68, June 1920, p. 687.
16. Compare Williams's *Autobiography*, pp. 332–34 and p. 265; the 1923 statement is found in Webster Schott, ed., *Imaginations* (New York: New Directions, 1971), p. 117.
17. *Autobiography*, p. 138.
18. In "Americanism and Localism," pp. 684–88.
19. *Collected Poems, Volume I*, p. 64.
20. See Henry M. Sayre, *The Visual Text of William Carlos Williams* (Urbana: University of Illinois Press, 1983).
21. "The Relations Between Poetry and Painting," in *The Necessary Angel: Essays on Reality and Imagination* (New York: Vintage, 1951), pp. 160–61.
22. *The Blind Man*, no. 2, May 1917, p. 15.
23. *The Visual Text*, p. 46.
24. Cited in Karen Tsujimoto, *Images of America: Precisionist Painting and Modern Photography* (Seattle: University of Washington Press for the San Francisco Museum of Art, 1982), p. 93.
25. *The Blind Man*, no. 2, May 1917, p. 5.
26. Williams dedicated *Spring and All* to Demuth. Demuth also sketched a poster for Stevens, *Study for Poster Portrait: Homage to Wallace Stevens*, although no painting was completed (Barbara Haskell, *Charles Demuth* [New York: Abrams, 1987] p. 178).
27. *Collected Poems, Volume I*, p. 174. Williams's "The Crimson Cyclamen" is also based on Demuth's paintings of flowers (see James E. Breslin, "William Carlos Williams and Charles Demuth: Cross-Fertilization in the Arts," *Journal of Modern Literature*, vol. 6, April 1977, pp. 248–63).
28. See Wanda Corn in *In the American Grain: The Billboard Poetics of Charles Demuth* (Poughkeepsie: Vassar College, The Agnes Rindge Claflin Endowment series, 1991), pp. 6–10.
29. *Imaginations*, pp. 105, 98; these descriptions come from *Spring and All* (dedicated to Demuth), in which Williams's most obviously "clean-lined," imagistic poems appeared.
30. Patricia C. Willis, ed., *The Complete Prose of Marianne Moore* (New York: Viking, 1986), p.191.
31. *America and Alfred Stieglitz*, pp. 29, 299. Most later critics side with Toomer; thus, for Corn, Demuth's "motion" is "futurist," not part of an aesthetic shared with Precisionism (*The Billboard Poetics*, p. 8),

while for Hilton Kramer, "Nothing *moves* in this [Precisionist] style. Everything is . . . *still*" ("The American Precisionists," *Arts Magazine*, vol. 35, March 1961, p. 37).

32. Strand, "Photography and the New God," *Broom*, vol. 3, November 1922, pp. 255–56.

33. "Comment," *Dial*, vol. 79, August 1925, p. 177; on the association between American culture and speed, see Cecelia Tichi, "Twentieth Century Limited: William Carlos Williams' Poetics of High Speed America," *The William Carlos Williams Review*, vol. 9, Fall 1983, pp. 49–72.

34. From *Spring and All*, in *Collected Poems, Volume I*, pp. 196–97.

35. Cited in Betsy Fahlman, *Pennsylvania Modern: Charles Demuth of Lancaster* (Philadelphia: Philadelphia Museum of Art, 1983), p. 22, from a January 16, 1926, letter to Stieglitz.

36. *Poetry*, vol. 37, February 1931, p. 268; the entire issue was guest edited by Louis Zukofsky, whose list of objectivist poems included also work by Eliot, cummings, McAlmon, and Reznikoff. Williams wrote the entry on "Objectivism" for *The Princeton Encyclopedia of Poetry and Poetics*, ed. Alex Preminger (Princeton: Princeton University Press, 1965), p. 582, saying the group originated in 1931, published "several books and, together, in 1932, an *Objectivist Anthology*." Williams continued: "The movement, never widely accepted, was early abandoned." Still, the writings of Zukofsky, Reznikoff, and Oppen—still known as objectivists—can be seen as related to the Precisionist movement.

37. January 10, 1938, letter to Constance Rourke; cited in *Williams: The American Background*, p. 62.

38. Cited in Carol Troyen and Erica E. Hirshler, *Charles Sheeler: Paintings and Drawings* (Boston: Boston Museum of Fine Arts, 1987), p. 142.

39. *The Collected Poems, Volume I*, pp. 444–45. For some debate on the relation between Williams's "Classic Scene" and Sheeler's *Classic Landscape*, see Bram Dijkstra, *The Hieroglyphics of a New Speech: Cubism, Stieglitz, and the Early Poetry of William Carlos Williams* (Princeton: Princeton University Press, 1969), p. 191; Stewart, "Charles Sheeler, William Carlos Williams, and Precisionism," p. 109; and *The Visual Text of William Carlos Williams*, p. 69, n. 24.

40. Dickran Tashjian, *Skyscraper Primitives: Dada and the American Avant-Garde* (Middletown, Connecticut: Wesleyan University Press, 1975), pp. 223–24, describes Williams's reading unintended social comment into Sheeler's landscapes.

41. Reprinted in Bram Dijkstra, ed., *A Recognizable Image: William Carlos Williams on Art and Artists* (New York: New Directions, 1978), pp. 146–48.

42. *Necessary Angel*, p. 34.

WORKS IN THE EXHIBITION

European Precedents

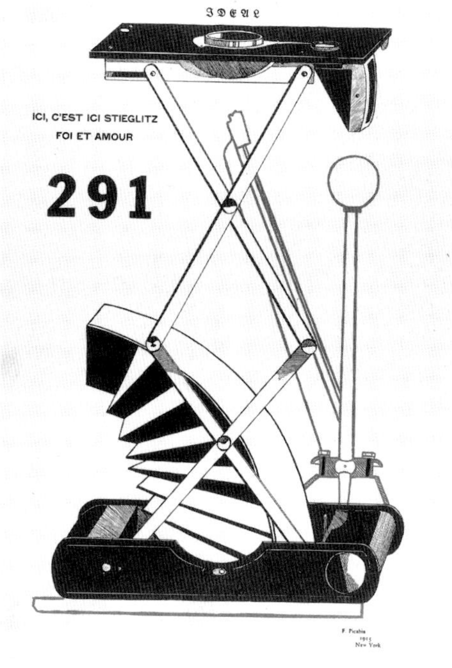

Right:
1. Francis Picabia. *Ici, c'est Stieglitz.* 1915. Double-sided cover for *291*, July–August. Lithograph, 17⅛ x 11⅜". Philadelphia Museum of Art. The Louise and Walter Arensberg Collection

Below:
2. Charles Sheeler. *Interior, Arensbergs' Apartment, New York.* ca. 1918. Casein silver print, 7⅝ x 9¾". Philadelphia Museum of Art. The Louise and Walter Arensberg Collection, 1950-134-989

Some of the key works of art in the Arensbergs' collection can be seen in the photograph. To the left, Duchamp's *Chocolate Grinder, No. 1,* 1913, hangs above Picabia's *Physical Culture,* 1913. In the center is Matisse's *Mlle Yvonne Landesberg,* 1914; to its right and over Sheeler's *Barn Abstraction,* 1918, hangs Georges Braque's *Musical Forms,* 1913.

Urban Views

3. Alfred Stieglitz. *View from the Rear Window, Gallery 291 at Night.* 1915. Platinum print, 10 × 8". Williams College Museum of Art, Williamstown, Massachusetts. Gift of John H. Rhoades, Class of 1934, 68.16

4. Alfred Stieglitz. *View from the Rear Window, Gallery 291, Daytime.* 1915. Platinum print, 10 × $7\frac{15}{16}$". Williams College Museum of Art, Williamstown, Massachusetts. Gift of John H. Rhoades, Class of 1934, 68.17

5. Paul Strand. *Wall Street, New York.* 1915. Photogravure, 11 ¼ x 7¾". Collection Centre Canadien d'Architecture/Canadian Centre for Architecture, Montréal. Copyright © 1971 Aperture Foundation Inc., Paul Strand Archive. Published as *New York* in *Camera Work*, no. 48, October 1916, plate 25

6. Morton Schamberg. *Untitled (Cityscape).* 1916. Gelatin silver print, 15 15⁄16 x 13". New Orleans Museum of Art. Museum Purchase, Women's Volunteer Committee Funds

7. Paul Strand. *New York.* 1917. Platinum print, 13⅜ x 10½". The Metropolitan Museum of Art, New York. The Alfred Stieglitz Collection, 1933, 33.43.335. Copyright © 1981 Aperture Foundation Inc., Paul Strand Archive

8. Charles Sheeler. *New York (Towards the Woolworth Building).* 1920. Gelatin silver print, 10 x 8". Collection George Eastman House, Rochester, New York

Based on Sheeler's experiences filming *Manhatta,* this print and plate 9, *New York (Temple Court),* feature the Park Row Building as seen from the Equitable Building at 120 Broadway.

9. Charles Sheeler. *New York (Temple Court).* 1920. Gelatin silver print, 10 x 8". Collection George Eastman House, Rochester, New York

TEMPLE COURT

10. Preston Dickinson. *Along the Harlem River.* 1922. Oil, pastel, and charcoal on paper, 12¾ x 18⅞". Sheldon Memorial Art Gallery, University of Nebraska–Lincoln. F. M. Hall Collection, 1954.H-349

11. Preston Dickinson. *Washington Bridge.* 1922. Pastel, chalk, ink, and graphite on paper, 19 x 12⅜". Collection The Newark Museum. Gift of Miss Cora Louise Hartshorn, 1951, 51.149

12. Charles Sheeler. *MacDougal Alley.* 1922. Oil on canvas, 23⅞ x 18⅛". Davison Art Center Collection, Wesleyan University, Middletown, Connecticut. Gift of Mrs. Charlotte Jordon, 1951

13. George Ault. *Loft Buildings, No. 2.* 1923. Oil on canvas, 24 × 18". Collection Lawrence J. Goldrich, Virginia Beach, Virginia

14. Paul Strand. *The Court, New York.* 1924. Gelatin silver print, $9\frac{7}{8} \times 7\frac{3}{8}$". The Art Institute of Chicago. Ada Turnbull Hertie Fund, 1980.66. Copyright © 1971 Aperture Foundation Inc., Paul Strand Archive

15. Louis Lozowick. *Cleveland.* 1924–26. Oil on canvas, 20 × 15". Edward J. Lenkin and Katherine L. Meier

Before his departure for Paris in 1920, Lozowick traveled to the urban-industrial centers that he would later depict in his fourteen paintings of ten American cities. With its railroad yards, smokestacks, grain elevators, and skyscrapers, *Cleveland* is a summation of American industry.

16. George Ault. *From Brooklyn Heights.* 1925. Oil on canvas, 30 x 20". Collection The Newark Museum. Purchase 1928, The General Fund, 28.102

17. Arnold Ronnebeck. *Wall Street.* 1925. Lithograph, 15¾ x 11¼". Courtesy Michael Rosenfeld Gallery, New York

18. Stefan Hirsch. *Mill Town.* n.d. Acquired 1925. Oil on canvas, 30 x 40½". The Phillips Collection, Washington, D.C.

19. Charles Sheeler. *Delmonico Building.* 1926. Lithograph, 14¼ x 19¼". The Metropolitan Museum of Art, New York. John B. Turner Fund, 1968, 68.728

20. Niles Spencer. *Buildings.* ca. 1924. Oil on canvas, 24 x 30". Columbus Museum of Art, Ohio. Gift of Ferdinand Howald, 31.268

21. Louis Lozowick. *Seattle.* ca. 1926–27. Oil on canvas, 30⅛ x 22⅛". Hirshhorn Museum and Sculpture Garden, Smithsonian Institution, Washington, D.C. Gift of Joseph H. Hirshhorn, 1966, 66.3122

22. Elsie Driggs. *Queensborough Bridge.* 1927. Oil on canvas, 40 x 30". The Montclair Art Museum, New Jersey. Lang Acquisition Fund, 69.4

23. Georgia O'Keeffe. *East River from the 30th Story of the Shelton Hotel.* 1928. Oil on canvas, 30 x 48". New Britain Museum of American Art, Connecticut. Stephen Lawrence Fund, 1958.9

24. Georgia O'Keeffe. *New York Night.* 1928–29. Oil on canvas, 40⅛ x 19⅛". Sheldon Memorial Art Gallery, University of Nebraska–Lincoln. Nebraska Art Association Collection, Thomas C. Woods Memorial Collection, 1958.N-107

25. Stefan Hirsch. *Night Terminal.* 1929. Oil on canvas, 22 5/16 x 29 3/16". The Regis Collection, Minneapolis, Minnesota

26. Louis Lozowick. *Brooklyn Bridge.* 1929. Lithograph, 13 1/16 × 7 7/8". Collection Françoise and Harvey Rambach

27. Louis Lozowick. *Hudson Bridge.* 1929. Lithograph, 14 3/8 × 8 11/16". Collection Françoise and Harvey Rambach

28. Howard Cook. *Chrysler Building.* 1930. Wood engraving, 10 × 6¾". Collection Françoise and Harvey Rambach

29. Ralston Crawford. *Near Wall Street.* ca. 1930s. Gelatin silver print, 3¼ x 2¼". Collection Foster and Monique Goldstrom, New York

30. Ernest Fiene. *Empire State Building.* 1930. Lithograph, 14 × 12". Collection Françoise and Harvey Rambach

31. Howard Cook. *George Washington Bridge.* 1931. Lithograph, $13\frac{13}{16} \times 9\frac{13}{16}$". The Metropolitan Museum of Art, New York. The Elisha Whittelsey Collection, The Elisha Whittelsey Fund, 1963, 63.509.6

32. Earl Horter. *The Chrysler Building Under Construction.* 1931. Ink and watercolor on paper, 20¼ x 14¾". Collection Whitney Museum of American Art, New York. Purchase, with funds from Mrs. William A. Marsteller, 78.17

33. Francis Criss. *Third Avenue El.* 1932. Oil on canvas, 14 x 18". Private Collection; courtesy Amy Wolf Fine Art, New York

34. Alfred Stieglitz. *Evening, New York from the Shelton.* 1932. Gelatin silver print, 9½ x 7$\frac{9}{16}$". Philadelphia Museum of Art. From the Collection of Dorothy Norman, 2-1975-60

35. Armin Landeck. *Manhattan Canyon.* 1934. Drypoint, 14 x 6¾". The DeWoody Collection

36. Wade White. *View from Studio Window.* 1934. Oil on canvas, 26 x 22". Collection William F. Stewart, Atlanta, Georgia; courtesy Janet Marqusee Fine Arts, New York

37. Francis Criss. *Jefferson Market Court House.* 1935. Oil on canvas, 35 x 23⅛". From the Collection of the Samuel P. Harn Museum of Art, University of Florida. Gift of William H. and Eloise Chandler

Industrial and Mechanical Subjects

38. Miklos Suba. *Brooklyn Street Corner.* 1939. Oil on canvas, 24 x 20". Courtesy James Graham & Sons, Inc., New York

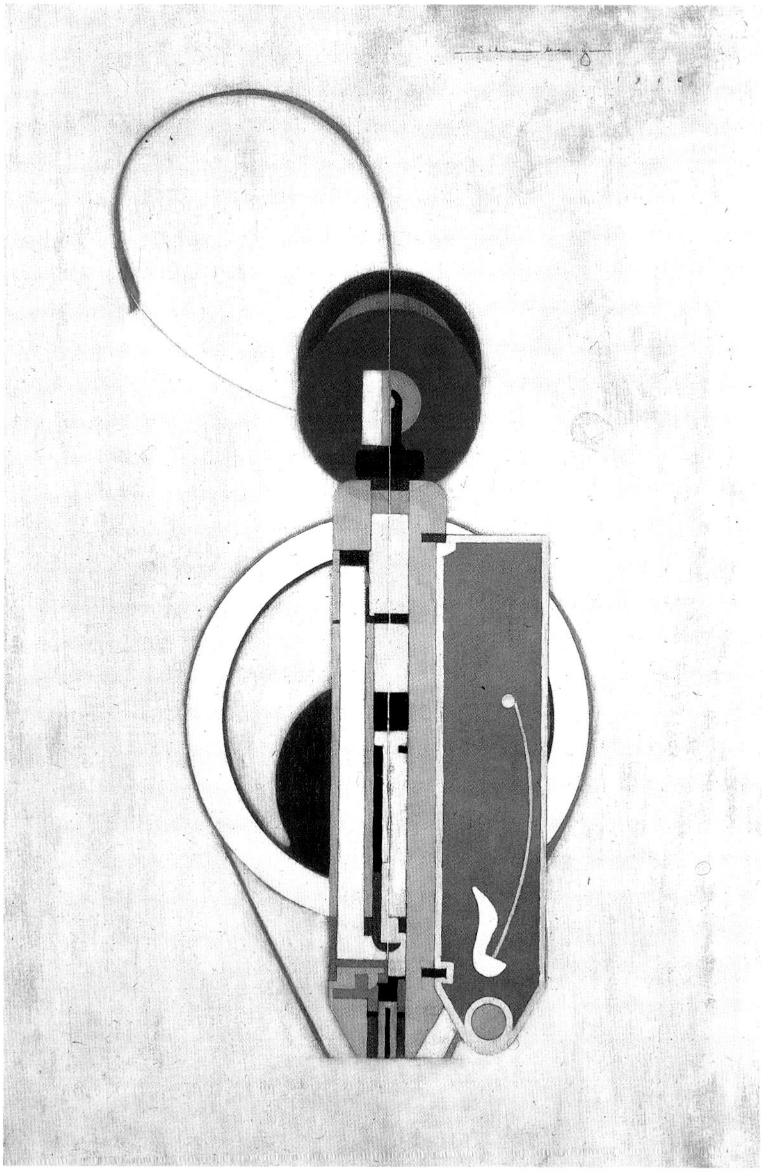

39. Morton Schamberg. *Mechanical Abstraction.* 1916. Oil on canvas, 30 x 20¼". Philadelphia Museum of Art. Louise and Walter Arensberg Collection, 50-134-18

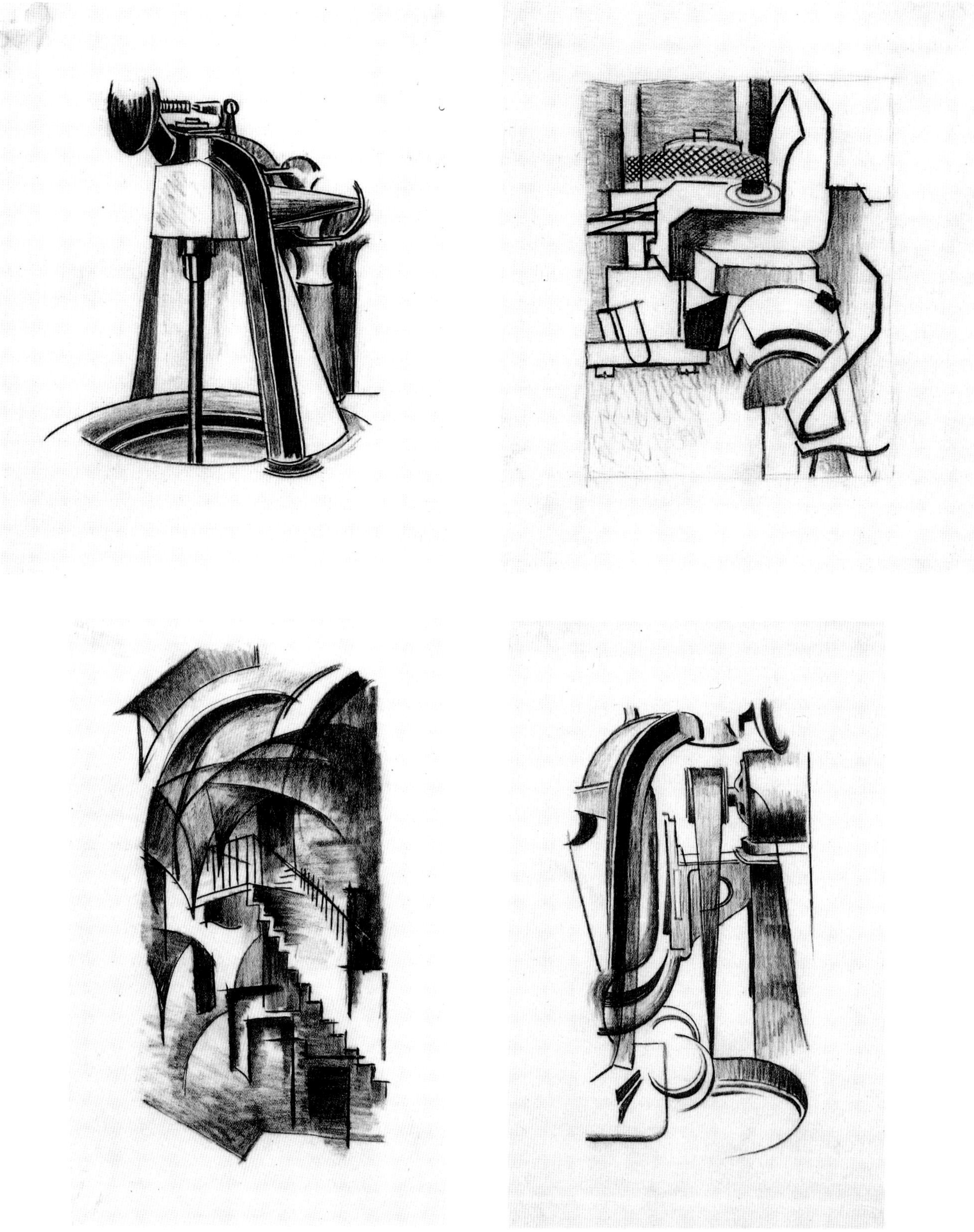

40. Morton Schamberg. *Untitled.* Four studies, including sketch for *Painting VII (The Well)*. ca. 1916. Pencil on paper, mounted together, #1 and #2, $5\frac{1}{2} \times 4\frac{1}{2}$" each; #3 and #4, $7\frac{1}{4} \times 4\frac{5}{8}$" each. The Metropolitan Museum of Art, New York. Purchase, Bertram F. and Susie Brummer Foundation, Inc. Gift, 1968, 68.115.1-4

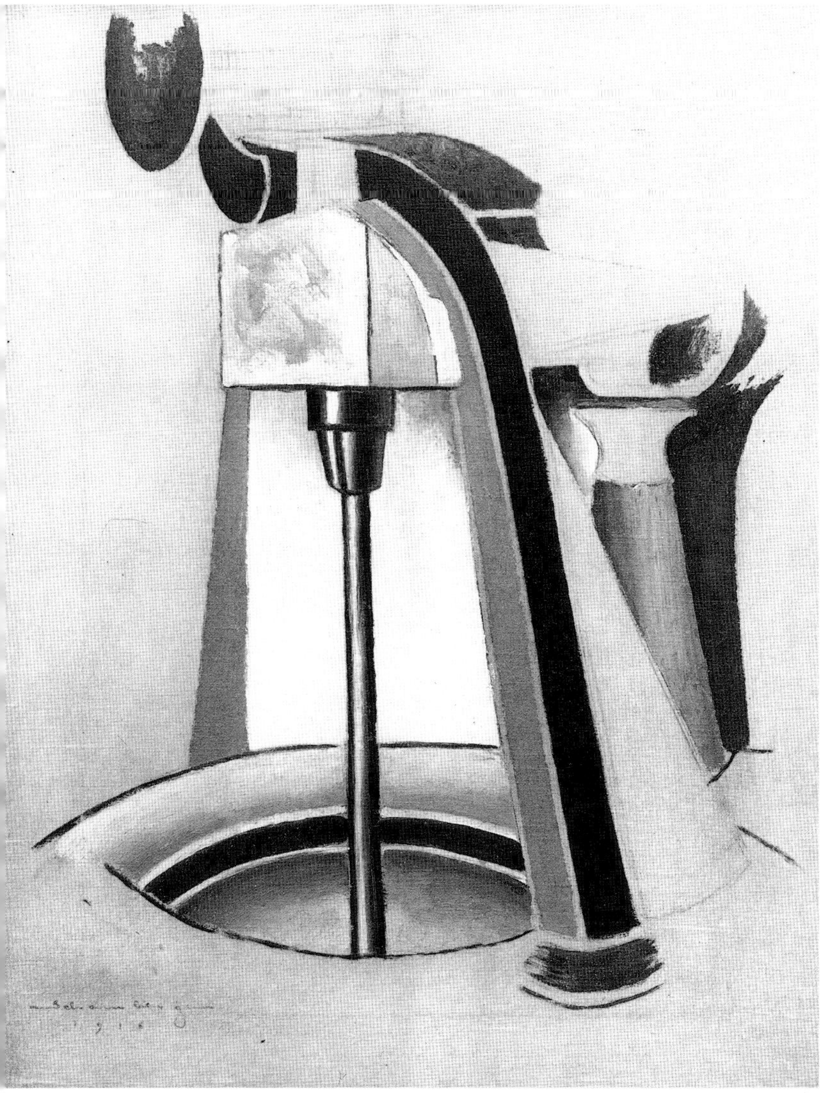

41. Morton Schamberg. *Painting VII (The Well).* 1916. Oil on canvas, 18⅛ x 14". Rose Art Museum, Brandeis University, Waltham, Massachusetts. Gift of Mr. Samuel Lustgarten

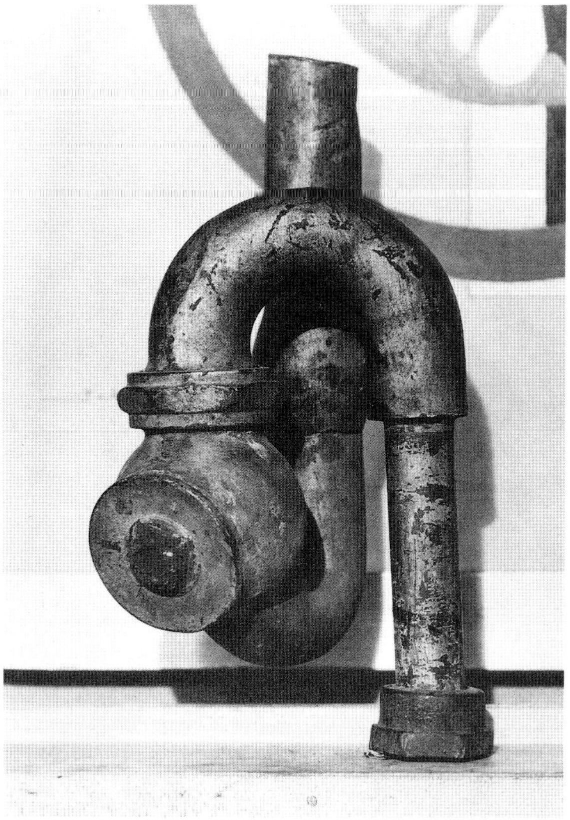

42. Morton Schamberg. *God.* ca. 1916. Gelatin silver print, 9½ x 7 9/16". The Metropolitan Museum of Art, New York. The Elisha Whittelsey Collection, The Elisha Whittelsey Fund, 1973.637

Akin to Duchamp's *Fountain* (fig. 27), this bitterly ironic Dadaist assemblage of plumbing pipes mounted on a miter box has been attributed to Schamberg, as assisted by another member of the Arensberg circle, Baroness Elsa von Freytag-Loringhoven. It has also been suggested that Schamberg was responsible for this photograph only and that the piece was executed entirely by the eccentric baroness.

43. Joseph Stella. *Telegraph Pole.* ca. 1920. Gouache and ink on paper, 24½ x 19½". Collection Mr. and Mrs. Meyer P. Potamkin

44. Joseph Stella. *Factories.* ca. 1921. Oil on burlap, 56 x 46". The Museum of Modern Art, New York. Acquired through the Lillie P. Bliss Bequest, 1943

45. Charles Demuth. *Aucassin and Nicolette.* 1921. Oil on canvas, 24⅛ x 20". Columbus Museum of Art, Ohio. Gift of Ferdinand Howald, 1931, 31.123

Demuth has transformed the hermetic, literary theme of medieval French star-crossed lovers into a nestling watertower and smokestack in his hometown, Lancaster, Pennsylvania.

46. Paul Strand. *Akeley Motion Picture Camera, New York.* 1923. Gelatin silver print, 10 x 8". Philadelphia Museum of Art. Gift of Hazel Strand and the Estate of Paul Strand. Copyright © 1971 Aperture Foundation Inc., Paul Strand Archive

47. Paul Strand. *Lathe, Akeley Shop, New York.* 1923. Gelatin silver print, 9¼ x 7⅜". Philadelphia Museum of Art. The Paul Strand Retrospective Collection: 1915–1975. Gift of the Estate of Paul Strand. Copyright © 1971 Aperture Foundation Inc., Paul Strand Archive

48. Paul Outerbridge. *Marmon Crankshaft.* 1923. Platinum print, 4½ x 3⅜". The Art Institute of Chicago. Julien Levy Collection, Gift of Jean and Julien Levy, 1975.1144. (Print in exhibition lent by the Gilman Paper Company Collection)

49. Paul Outerbridge. *Electric Lightbulbs.* 1923. Platinum print, 4 x 3½". Courtesy Ezra Mack, New York

50. Preston Dickinson. *Industry.* ca. 1923. Oil on canvas, 30 x 24¼". Collection Whitney Museum of American Art, New York. Gift of Gertrude Vanderbilt Whitney

51. Preston Dickinson. *Grain Elevators.* 1924. Pastel and graphite on paper, 24⅝ x 17¾". Columbus Museum of Art, Ohio. Gift of Ferdinand Howald, 1931, 31.154

52. Edward Weston. *Plaster Works.* 1925. Gelatin silver print, 7 15/16 x 9 15/16". The Art Museum, Princeton University, New Jersey. Gift of David H. McAlpin

Below:
53. George Ault. *Brooklyn Ice House.* 1926. Oil on canvas, 24 x 30". Collection The Newark Museum. Purchase 1928, The General Fund, 28.1760

54. Charles Sheeler. *Bleeder Stacks, Ford Plant.* 1927. Gelatin silver print, 9½ x 7½". The Museum of Modern Art, New York. Gift of Samuel M. Kootz

55. Charles Sheeler. *Pulverizer Building, Ford Plant, Detroit.* 1927. Gelatin silver print, 9⅜ x 7⅜". The Museum of Modern Art, New York. Gift of Lincoln Kirstein

56. Charles Sheeler. *Slag Buggy, Ford Plant, Detroit.* 1927. Gelatin silver print, $8\frac{7}{8} \times 7\frac{1}{2}$". The Museum of Modern Art, New York. Gift of Lincoln Kirstein

57. Charles Sheeler. *Criss-Crossed Conveyors, Ford Plant.* 1927 (print ca. 1970 by Gerda Peterich). Gelatin silver print, $10\frac{1}{2} \times 9\frac{3}{8}$". Collection George Eastman House, Rochester, New York

58. Elsie Driggs. *Pittsburgh.* 1927. Oil on canvas, 34¼ x 40". Collection Whitney Museum of American Art, New York. Gift of Gertrude Vanderbilt Whitney

59. Peter Blume. *White Factory.* 1928. Oil on canvas, 20⅛ x 30⅛". Sheldon Memorial Art Gallery, University of Nebraska–Lincoln. Nebraska Art Association, Nelle Cochrane Woods Memorial Collection, 1957.N-98

60. Henry Billings. *White Boats.* 1929. Tempera on board, 26½ x 44". Private Collection

61. Louis Lozowick. *Machine Ornament No. 2.* 1927. Ink on paper, 11½ x 18". Collection Françoise and Harvey Rambach

62. Imogen Cunningham. *Shredded Wheat Tower.* 1928. Gelatin silver print, 9 x 6½". The Metropolitan Museum of Art, New York. Ford Motor Company and John C. Waddell, 1987.1100.95. Photograph by Imogen Cunningham copyright © 1978, 1993

63. Niles Spencer. *White Factory.* 1928. Lithograph, 10½ x 13¾".
Collection Françoise and Harvey Rambach

64. Ralph Steiner. *Ford Model T.* ca. 1929. Gelatin silver print, 7⅛ x 9⅝".
Courtesy Howard Greenberg Gallery, New York

65. Charles Sheeler. *Classic Landscape.* 1931. Oil on canvas, 25 x 32¼".
Mr. and Mrs. Barney A. Ebsworth Foundation

66. Ralph Steiner. *Portrait of Louis Lozowick.* 1930. Gelatin silver print, 10 x 7½". Collection Adele Lozowick

67. Elsie Driggs. *Aeroplane.* 1928. Oil on canvas, 44 x 38". Private Collection

During her first flight on a Ford trimotor plane from Cleveland to Detroit, where she intended to explore the River Rouge plant, Driggs was invited to sit with the captain. Thrilled with the new sensation of flying, she later made numerous studies of the plane itself, resulting in this Precisionist tour de force.

68. Louis Lozowick. *Relic.* ca. 1929–30. Carbon pencil on paper, 14½ x 8⅛". New Jersey State Museum Collection. Purchase FA1966.60

69. Peter Blume. *Coal Breaker—Scranton.* 1930. Pencil on paper, 9⅛ x 11⅞". The Metropolitan Museum of Art, New York. Rogers Fund, 1953, 53.26

70. Edward Bruce. *Industry.* 1932. Oil on canvas, 28 x 36". Collection Whitney Museum of American Art, New York. Exchange

71. Charles Demuth. *After All.* 1933. Oil on board, 36 x 30". Collection Norton Gallery of Art, West Palm Beach, Florida. 53.43

Demuth's final oil painting was titled after a poem by Walt Whitman, "After All, Not to Create Only," which celebrated American industry. The subject of this painting—Demuth's last major architectural or industrial work—was based on Lancaster's Armstrong Cork Company complex.

72. Imogen Cunningham. *Fageol Ventilators, Oakland, California.* 1934. Gelatin silver print, 7⅛ x 9". Collection Edward J. Lenkin and Katherine L. Meier. Photograph by Imogen Cunningham copyright © 1970, 1993

73. Arnold Wiltz. *Construction on the Hudson.* 1934. Oil on canvas, 22½ x 30". Private Collection; courtesy D. Wigmore Fine Art, Inc., New York

74. Miklos Suba. *Ship's Funnels.* 1932. Graphite and blue pencil on white paper, 12 x 9". The Metropolitan Museum of Art, New York. Rogers Fund, 1958, 58.69

75. Ralston Crawford. *Ventilator with Porthole.* 1935. Oil on canvas, 40 x 34". Sheldon Memorial Art Gallery, University of Nebraska–Lincoln. F. M. Hall Collection, 1975.H-2247

76. Virginia Berresford. *City of Factories.* 1937. Oil on canvas, 30½ × 48". Courtesy Michael Rosenfeld Gallery, New York

77. Ralston Crawford. *Buffalo Grain Elevators.* 1937. Oil on canvas, 40¼ × 50¼". National Museum of American Art, Smithsonian Institution, Washington, D.C., 1976.133

78. Ralston Crawford. *Buffalo Grain Elevators with Tension Wires.* ca. 1938. Gelatin silver print, 3 × 5". The Metropolitan Museum of Art, New York. Ford Motor Company Collection, Gift of the Ford Motor Company and John C. Waddell, 1987.1100.441

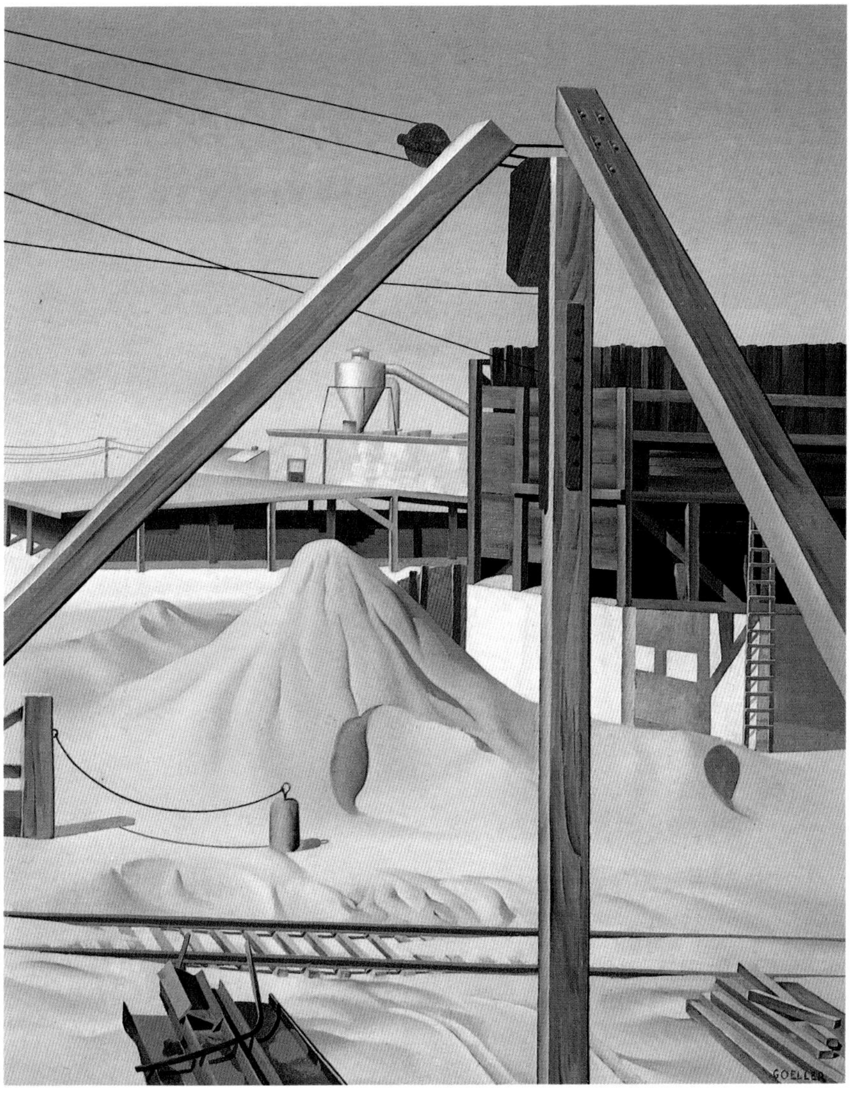

79. Charles Goeller. *Factory Yard.* ca. 1938. Oil on canvas, 43 × 34". Collection of The Newark Museum. Bequest of the artist, 1955, 55.104

80. Ralston Crawford. *Sanford Tanks No. 2.* 1939. Oil on canvas, 28 × 36". Collection Arthur E. Imperatore; courtesy Luhring Augustine Gallery, New York

81. Edmund Lewandowski. *Industrial Composition.* 1939. Watercolor on paper, 22 × 30". The Brooklyn Museum. Dick S. Ramsay Fund, 41.513

82. Edmund Lewandowski. *Insulators.* 1939. Conté crayon and pencil, 23 × 18½". The Regis Collection, Minneapolis, Minnesota

83. Charles Sheeler. *Suspended Power.* 1939. Oil on canvas, 33 x 26". Dallas Museum of Art. Gift of Edmund J. Kahn

Commissioned and published by *Fortune* magazine in December 1940, this painting depicts a monumental hydraulic turbine generator at a hydroelectric plant in Alabama. The generator is about to be lowered into its pit, seemingly threatening to eliminate the minuscule, anonymous workers below.

84. Niles Spencer. *Waterfront Mill.* 1940. Oil on canvas, 30 x 36". The Metropolitan Museum of Art, New York. Arthur Hoppock Hearn Fund, 1942, 42.169

Above:

85. Charles Sheeler. *Yankee Clipper.* 1939. Oil on canvas, 24 x 28". Museum of Art, Rhode Island School of Design, Providence. Jesse Metcalf and Mary B. Jackson Funds, 41.006

This painting was also published in *Fortune* in December 1940. Sheeler was characterized as expressing "the new portent [of man's] adventure in space" in his sleek, elegant depiction of the airplane's "poised and infinitely precise propeller, aimed at the sky."

86. Edward Weston. *Santa Fe, New York.* 1941. Gelatin silver print, 7 x 9". Courtesy Ezra Mack, New York

Still Lifes

87. Charles Sheeler. *Zinnia and Nasturtium Leaves.* ca. 1915–17. Gelatin silver print, 9⅝ x 7¹¹⁄₁₆". Worcester Art Museum, Massachusetts. Anonymous gift

88. Paul Strand. *Still Life: Jug and Fruit, Twin Lakes, Connecticut.* 1915. Gelatin silver print, 13⁹⁄₁₆ x 9¾". Philadelphia Museum of Art. Gift of Hazel Strand and the Estate of Paul Strand. Copyright © Aperture Foundation, Inc., Paul Strand Archive

89. Morton Schamberg. *Bowl of Flowers*. 1918. Watercolor and pencil on paper, 12⅛ x 9⅛". National Museum of American Art, Smithsonian Institution, Washington, D.C. Bequest of Jean L. Whitehill, 1986.27

90. Preston Dickinson. *Still Life with Compote*. 1922. Pastel on paper, 15½ x 18". Collection Norton Gallery of Art, West Palm Beach, Florida, 80.22

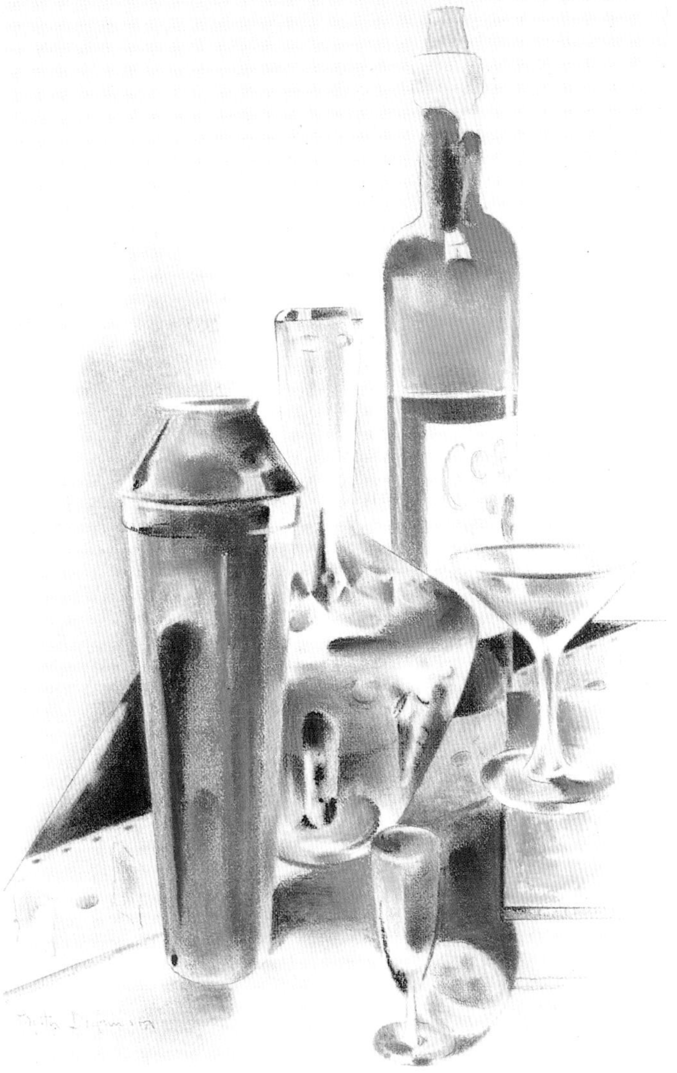

91. Preston Dickinson. *Hospitality.* 1925. Pastel on paper, 21¼ x 13½". Columbus Museum of Art, Ohio. Gift of Ferdinand Howald, 1931, 31.157

92. Charles Sheeler. *Gloxinia.* 1923. Pastel on paper, 23¼ x 19¼". Collection Françoise and Harvey Rambach

93. Charles Sheeler. *Still Life and Shadows.* 1924. Conté crayon, watercolor, and tempera on paper, 31 x 21". Columbus Museum of Art, Ohio. Gift of Ferdinand Howald, 1931, 31.106

94. Stuart Davis. *Roses in Vase.* 1924. Oil on board, 24½ x 18¼". Courtesy Salander O'Reilly Galleries, New York

Below:
95. Niles Spencer. *Interior: Still Life.* 1925. Oil on canvas, 28 x 28". The Regis Collection, Minneapolis, Minnesota

96. Charles Demuth. *Still Life with Spoon.* 1927. Gouache with graphite on academy board, 11⅝ x 9½". Georgia Museum of Art, University of Georgia, Athens, Eva Underhill Holbrook Memorial Collection of American Art. Gift of Alfred H. Holbrook, GMOA 47.156

Below:
97. Charles Demuth. *Eggplant, Carrots, and Tomatoes.* 1927. Watercolor on paper, 13⅞ x 19⅞". Collection Norton Gallery of Art, West Palm Beach, Florida

98. Georgia O'Keeffe. *Peach and Glass.* 1927. 9 × 6". Philadelphia Museum of Art. Gift of Dr. Herman Lorber

99. George Ault. *Mantelpiece Composition.* 1929. Oil on canvas, 16 × 14". Collection Françoise and Harvey Rambach

100. Louis Lozowick. *Still Life No. 2.* 1929. Lithograph, 10 5/16 x 13 3/16". Collection Françoise and Harvey Rambach

Right:
101. Rosella Hartman. *Still Life, Flowers and Fruit.* 1930. Pen and ink on paper, 19 x 15". Private Collection; courtesy Conner-Rosenkranz, New York

102. Stefan Hirsch. *Tulips.* ca. 1930. Pencil on paper, 15 1/2 x 20". Courtesy Conner-Rosenkranz, New York

103. Niles Spencer. *The Green Table.* 1930. Oil on canvas, 50 × 40".
Collection Whitney Museum of American Art, New York. Purchase

104. Charles Sheeler. *Cactus.* 1931. Oil on canvas, 45⅛ x 30". Philadelphia Museum of Art. Louise and Walter Arensberg Collection, 50-134-186

105. Charles Demuth. *Pink Magnolias.* 1933. Watercolor and pencil on paper, 9⅞ x 13⅞". Collection Françoise and Harvey Rambach

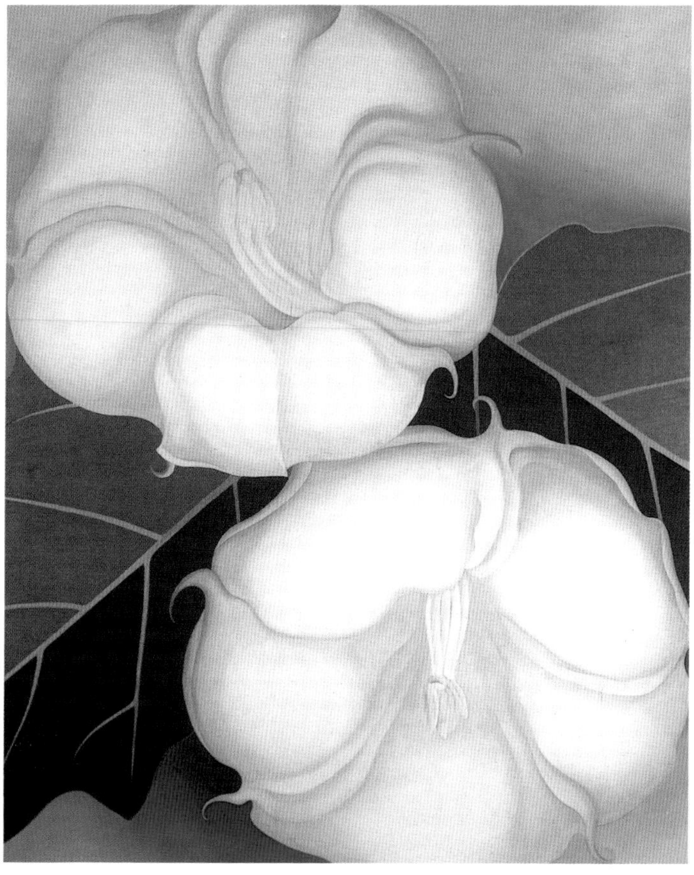

106. Georgia O'Keeffe. *Two Jimson Weeds with Green Leaves and Blue Sky.* 1938. Oil on canvas, 48 x 40". Collection Françoise and Harvey Rambach

Rural Vernacular Architecture and Americana

107. Charles Sheeler. *Side of White Barn.* ca. 1916–17. Gelatin silver print, 8 x 10". Gilman Paper Company Collection

108. Paul Strand. *The White Fence, Port Kent, New York.* 1916. Photogravure, 6 11/16 x 8 11/16". Private Collection. Copyright © 1971 Aperture Foundation Inc., Paul Strand Archive

Above:
109. Charles Demuth. *Bermuda, No. 1, Tree and House.* 1917. Watercolor on paper, 10 x 13⅞". The Metropolitan Museum of Art, New York. The Alfred Stieglitz Collection, 1949, 49.70.55

110. Charles Sheeler. *Bucks County Barn.* 1917. Gelatin silver print, 7 x 9". Collection Marjorie S. and Leonard Vernon

111. Charles Demuth. *Red-Roofed Houses*. 1917. Watercolor and graphite on paper, $9\frac{3}{4}$ x 14". Philadelphia Museum of Art. The Samuel S. White 3rd and Vera White Collection, 67-30-25

112. Charles Demuth. *Housetops.* 1918. Watercolor on paper, 9¾ x 13½". Columbus Museum of Art, Ohio. Gift of Ferdinand Howald, 1931, 31.134

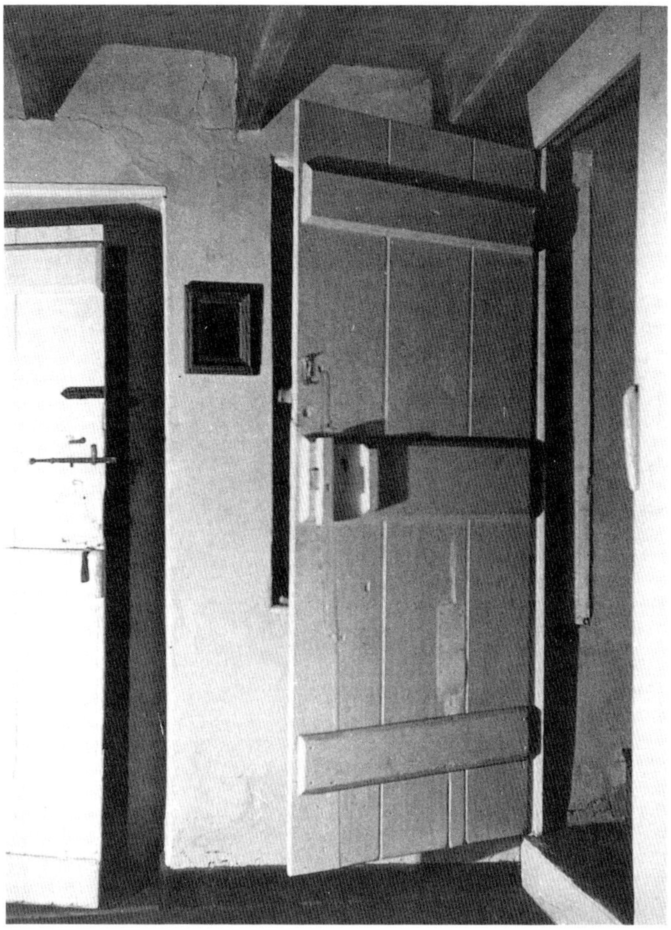

113. Charles Sheeler. *The Open Door.* ca. 1917. Gelatin silver print, 10 × 8". Courtesy Amon Carter Museum, Fort Worth, Texas

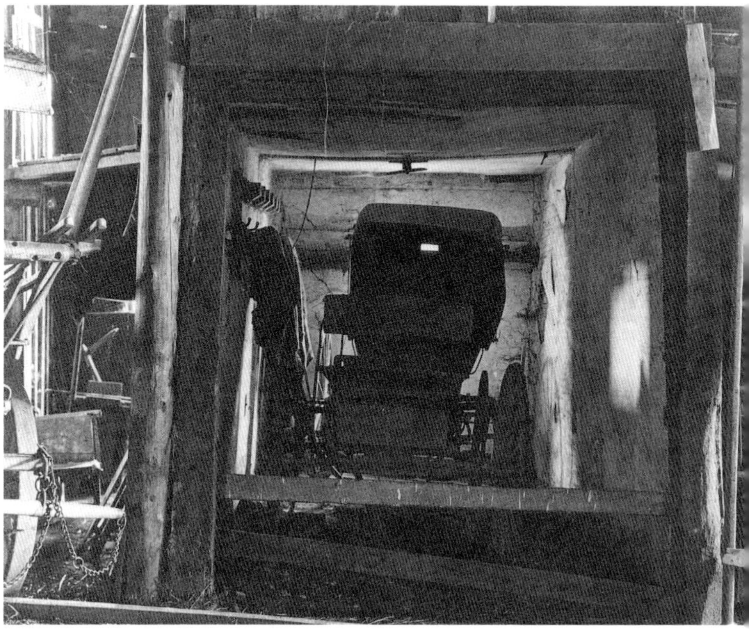

114. Charles Sheeler. *Interior, Bucks County Barn.* ca. 1917. Gelatin silver print, 7¾ × 9$^{11}/_{16}$". Sheldon Memorial Art Gallery, University of Nebraska–Lincoln. F. M. Hall Collection, H-2164

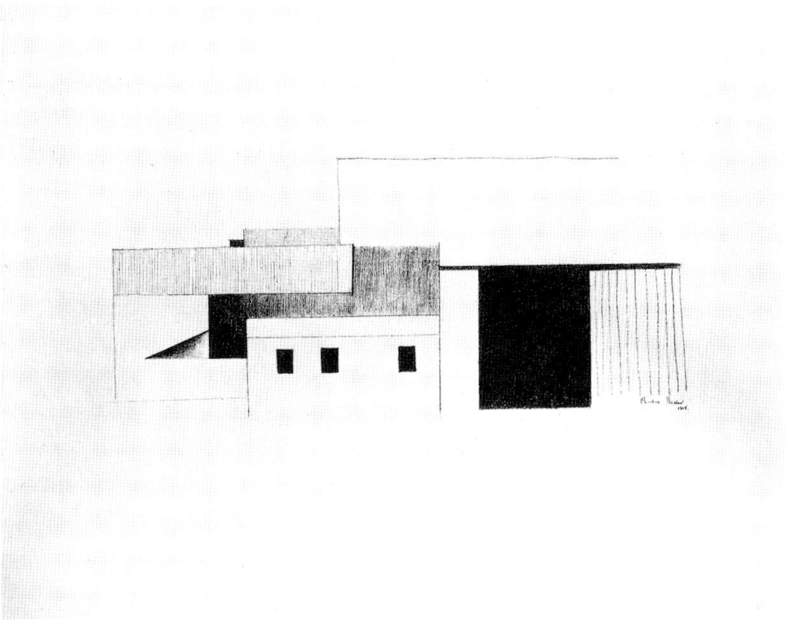

115. Charles Sheeler. *Barn Abstraction.* 1918. Lithograph, 22 x 28". The Metropolitan Museum of Art, New York. Rogers Fund, 1974, 74.501.1

116. Alfred Stieglitz. *Untitled (Barn, Lake George).* ca. 1921. Gelatin silver print, 7½ x 9⅜". Philadelphia Museum of Art. From the Collection of Dorothy Norman, 1976.212.002

Above:
117. Charles Sheeler. *Bucks County Barn.* 1918. Gouache and Conté crayon on paper, 16⅛ x 22⅛". Columbus Museum of Art, Ohio. Gift of Ferdinand Howald, 1931, 31.101

118. Niles Spencer. *The Cove.* 1922. Oil on canvas, 28 x 36". Collection The Newark Museum. Purchase 1926, The General Fund, 26.4

The title refers to Perkins Cove, Ogunquit, Maine. There Spencer and others absorbed European modernism and American folk art while working in rented houses or fishing shacks owned by Hamilton Easter Field, head of the town's progressive art colony.

120. Stuart Davis. *Street Scene.* 1926. Watercolor on paper, 11¼ x 16". New Jersey State Museum Collection. Gift of the Friends of the New Jersey State Museum, Trenton. Members Choice, FA1975.16

Above:
119. Niles Spencer. *New England Houses.* 1924. Oil on canvas, 22¼ x 35¼". Albright-Knox Art Gallery, Buffalo, New York. Charles W. Goodyear Fund, 1927

Above:
121. Peter Blume. *Winter, New Hampshire.* 1927. Oil on canvas, 20¼ x 25". Courtesy Museum of Fine Arts, Boston. Bequest of John T. Spaulding

122. Ralph Steiner. *American Rural Baroque.* ca. 1928 (1976 print). Gelatin silver print, 7½ x 9½". Collection Marjorie S. and Leonard Vernon

123. Howard Cook. *New England Church.* 1931. Wood engraving. 11 7/16 x 8 7/16". The Metropolitan Museum of Art, New York. Gift of Miss Marie L. Russell, 1942, 42.8.3

124. Georgia O'Keeffe. *Stables.* 1932. Oil on canvas, 12 x 32". The Detroit Institute of Arts. Gift of Robert H. Tannahill

Above:
125. Charles Sheeler. *Bucks County Barn.* 1932. Oil on gesso on composition board, 23⅞ x 29⅞". The Museum of Modern Art, New York. Gift of Abby Aldrich Rockefeller, 1935

126. Edmund Lewandowski. *Red Barn.* 1935. Watercolor on paper, 20 x 27". Sheldon Memorial Art Gallery, University of Nebraska–Lincoln. Allocation of the U.S. Government Federal Art Project of the Works Progress Administration, 1943 WPA-124

127. Charles Sheeler. *American Interior.* 1934. Oil on canvas, 32½ x 30".
Yale University Art Gallery, New Haven. Gift of Mrs. Paul Moore

128. Alfred Stieglitz. *Later Lake George.* 1934. Chloride print, 9¼ x 7¼". The Art Institute of Chicago. Alfred Stieglitz Collection, 1949.764

129. Charles Sheeler. *American Interior.* 1935. Watercolor and pencil on cardboard, 14¼ x 16". The Metropolitan Museum of Art, New York. George A. Hearn Fund, 1941, 41.178.1

Here Sheeler highlights the unadorned functional clarity and progressive precision of a Shaker wood stove.

130. Charles Sheeler. *American Interior (with Stove).* ca. 1932–35. Gelatin silver print, 7 x 9". The Art Museum, Princeton University, New Jersey. Museum purchase, Fowler McCormick Fund, x1980-13

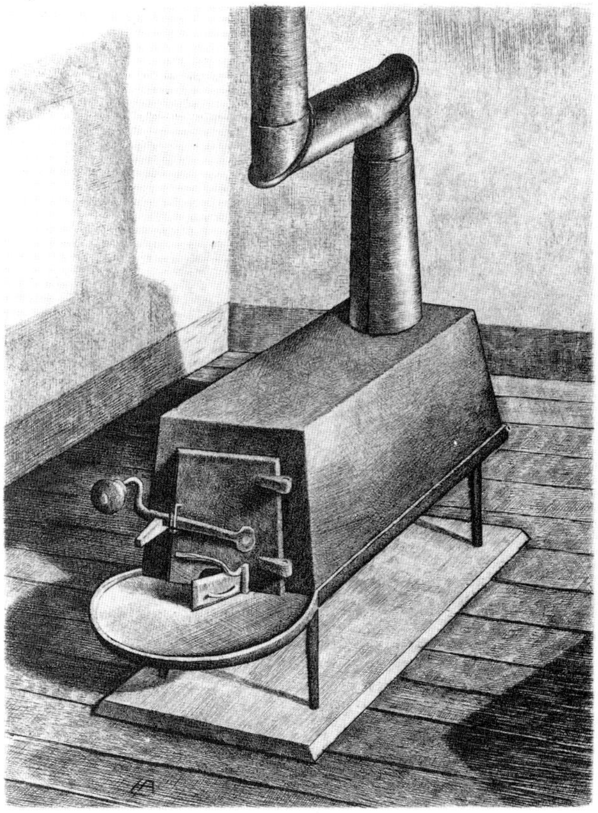

131. Armin Landeck. *Shaker Stove.* 1938. Drypoint, 8 x 5⅞". Courtesy The Old Print Shop Inc., New York

132. Ralston Crawford. *White Barn.* 1936. Oil on canvas, 30 × 36¼". Albright-Knox Art Gallery, Buffalo, New York. Room of Contemporary Art Fund, 1941

Above:
133. George Ault. *Studio Interior.* 1938. Watercolor and pencil on paper, 20 × 23⁹⁄₁₆". National Museum of American Art, Smithsonian Institution, Washington, D.C. Transfer from Museum of Modern Art, 1971.447.4

This view of Ault's Woodstock studio reveals his abiding appreciation of Americana.

134. George Ault. *Rick's Barn, Woodstock.* 1939. Gouache on paper, 18 × 25½". Columbus Museum of Art, Ohio. Gift of Louise Ault, 1961, 61.90

135. Charles Sheeler. *Shaker Detail.* 1941. Oil and tempera on Masonite, 9 x 10". Collection The Newark Museum. Wallace M. Scudder Bequest Fund, Purchase 1944, 44.169

136. Charles Sheeler. *Farm Buildings, Connecticut.* 1941. Tempera on cardboard, 16 x 21½". Collection The Newark Museum. Wallace M. Scudder Bequest Fund, Purchase 1944, 44.170

137. Edward Weston. *Connecticut Barn.* 1941. Gelatin silver print, 7 x 9". Collection Marjorie S. and Leonard Vernon

THE FOLLOWING WORKS IN THE EXHIBITION ARE NOT ILLUSTRATED:

138. George Ault. *Dahlia.* 1930. Watercolor on paper, $17\frac{1}{2} \times 11\frac{3}{4}$". Collection Françoise and Harvey Rambach

139. Howard Cook. *Begonia (Study for Lithograph).* 1929. Ink on paper, 12 x 16". Collection Françoise and Harvey Rambach

140. Ralston Crawford. *Grain Elevators, Wires, Lamp Shadows.* ca. 1930s. Gelatin silver print, 3 x 5". The Metropolitan Museum of Art, New York. Ford Motor Company Collection, Gift of the Ford Motor Company and John C. Waddell, 1987.1100.490

141. Charles Demuth. *Houses with Red.* 1917. Watercolor on paper, 10 x 14". The Metropolitan Museum of Art, New York. The Alfred Stieglitz Collection, 1949, 49.70.61

142. Charles Demuth. *Rooftops (Provincetown).* 1918. Watercolor on paper, 10 x 14". Collection Mr. and Mrs. Meyer P. Potamkin

143. Charles Demuth. *Trees and Barns, Bermuda.* 1917. Watercolor over graphite on paper, $9\frac{1}{2} \times 13\frac{7}{16}$". Williams College Museum of Art, Williamstown, Massachusetts. Bequest of Susan Watts Street, 57.8

144. Preston Dickinson. *The Bridge (Highbridge).* ca. 1922–23. Pastel, gouache, and graphite on paper, $19 \times 12\frac{3}{8}$". Collection The Newark Museum. Purchase 1930, The General Fund

145. Preston Dickinson. *Factories.* n.d. Gouache and graphite on paper, 16 x 9". Collection The Newark Museum. Gift of Mrs. Gustav Koven and Family, 1992

146. Elsie Driggs. *Study for "Pittsburgh."* 1927. Graphite on paper, $12 \times 14\frac{1}{2}$". Collection Whitney Museum of American Art, New York. 50th Anniversary Gift of Mr. and Mrs. Julian Foss

147. Marcel Duchamp. *Box in a Valise (Boîte-en-valise).* 1935–41. Mixed media, edition of thirty (1963 edition), box (closed) $14\frac{13}{16} \times 15\frac{15}{16} \times 3\frac{9}{16}$". Bonk series E, Lebel 173, Schwartz 311. The David and Alfred Smart Museum of Art, The University of Chicago. Gift of Mrs. Robert B. Mayer

148. Stefan Hirsch. *One Way Street.* 1929. Lithograph, $11\frac{5}{26} \times 15\frac{7}{8}$". Amon Carter Museum, Fort Worth, Texas

149. Earl Horter. *View of Hotel Pierre, New York.* ca. 1928. Pencil on paper, 22 x 28". The Metropolitan Museum of Art, New York

150. Francis Picabia. *Le Saint des Saints.* 1915. Double-sided cover for *291*, July–August. Lithograph, $17\frac{1}{8} \times 11\frac{3}{8}$". Philadelphia Museum of Art. Louise and Walter Arensberg Collection

151. Charles Sheeler. *Industrial Series No. 1.* 1928. Lithograph, $14\frac{1}{4} \times 19\frac{1}{4}$". The Metropolitan Museum of Art, New York. John B. Turner Fund, 1966, 66.593

152. Charles Sheeler. *New York (Buildings in Shadows).* 1920. Gelatin silver print, 10 x 8". Collection George Eastman House, Rochester, New York.

153. Charles Sheeler. *Criss-Crossed Conveyors, Ford Plant.* 1927. Gelatin silver print, $8\frac{7}{8} \times 7\frac{1}{2}$". The Museum of Modern Art, New York. Purchase

154. Charles Sheeler. *Upper Deck.* ca. 1928 (reproduction print by Richard Benson, 1985). Halftone print, 10 x 8". Gilman Paper Company Collection

155. Ralph Steiner. *Baker Coconut Factory, New York City.* ca. 1935. Gelatin silver print, $9\frac{1}{2} \times 7\frac{1}{4}$". The Art Museum, Princeton University, New Jersey. Museum purchase, gift of the National Endowment for the Arts, a federal agency, and an anonymous matching gift, x1974-144

SELECTED BIBLIOGRAPHY

Entries are arranged chronologically.

"Charles Sheeler–New Art Circle," *The Art News*, vol. 24, January 23, 1926, p. 7.

Phillips, Duncan, *A Collection in the Making*, New York: E. Weyhe, 1926.

Kalonyme, Louis, "Whitney Studio Club Members Exhibit Their Work," *The New York Times*, February 27, 1927, sec. 7, p. 11.

Barr, Alfred H., Jr., "Tendencies in Modern American Painting" (summary of lecture), *Bowdoin Orient*, May 11, 1927, pp. 3–4.

Lozowick, Louis, "The Americanization of Art," *Machine Age Exposition*, New York: *Little Review*, 1927, pp. 18–19.

Jewell, Edward Alden, "Galleries Offer Rich Display," *The New York Times*, October 14, 1928, p. 13.

"Immaculate School Seen at Daniel's," *The Art News*, vol. 22, November 3, 1928, p. 9.

Barr, Alfred H., Jr., "American Art Has Numerous Styles" (summary of lecture), *Wellesley College News*, May 9, 1929, p. 2.

Kootz, Samuel, *Modern American Painters*, New York: Brewer and Warren, Inc., 1930.

Mumford, Lewis, *The Brown Decades: A Study of the Arts in America 1865–1895*, New York: Harcourt, Brace, and Company, 1931, pp. 232–35, 241–45.

Cahill, Holger, "American Art Today," in *America as Americans See It*, New York: The Literary Guild, 1932, p. 258.

Index of Twentieth Century Artists, 4 vols., New York: College Art Association, 1933–37.

Cahill, Holger, and Alfred H. Barr Jr., *Art in America: A Complete Survey*, New York: Reynal & Hitchcock, 1935, pp. 95–99.

Barr, Alfred H., Jr., "Painting and Sculpture," *Trois Siècles d'art aux États-Unis*. Exh. cat. Paris: Éditions des Musées Nationaux, 1938, p. 29.

Boswell, Peyton, *Modern American Painting*, New York: Dodd, Mead, & Company, 1939, p. 105.

Cheney, Martha Candler, *Modern Art in America*, New York: Whittesley House, 1939, pp. 64–65.

Cheney, Sheldon, *The Story of Modern Art*, New York: The Viking Press, 1941, pp. 611–13.

Cincinnati Modern Art Society, *A New Realism: Crawford, Demuth, Sheeler, Spencer*. Exh. cat. Ohio: Cincinnati Art Museum, 1941.

Miller, Dorothy C., and Alfred H. Barr Jr., eds., *American Realists and Magic Realists*. Exh. cat. New York: The Museum of Modern Art, 1943, pp. 6, 8, 23, 28, 44–47, 56.

Brown, Milton, "Cubist-Realism: An American Style," *Marsyas*, vol. 3, 1943–45, pp. 139–60.

Born, Wolfgang, *Still-Life Painting in America*, New York: Oxford University Press, 1947, pp. 44–48.

Born, Wolfgang, *American Landscape Painting*, New Haven: Yale University Press, 1948, pp. 206–11.

Baur, John I. H., *Revolution and Tradition in Modern American Art*, Cambridge, Massachusetts: Harvard University Press, 1951.

Brown, Milton, *American Painting from the Armory Show to the Depression*, Princeton: Princeton University Press, 1955.

"The Precisionists," *Art in America*, vol. 48, Fall 1960. Special issue with four articles:

> Andrews, Edward Deming, "The Shaker Manner of Building," pp. 38–45.
>
> Arnason, H. H., "The New Geometry," pp. 54–61.
>
> Friedman, Martin, "The Precisionist View," pp. 30–37.
>
> Scully, Vincent J., Jr., "The Precisionist Strain in American Architecture," pp. 46–53.

Friedman, Martin, *The Precisionist View in American Art*. Exh. cat. Minneapolis: Walker Art Center, 1960.

Kramer, Hilton, "The American Precisionists," *Arts*, vol. 35, March 1961, pp. 32–37.

Celender, Donald Dennis, "Precisionism in Twentieth-Century American Painting," Ph.D. diss., University of Pittsburgh, 1963.

Adams, Clinton, *Cubism: Its Impact in the USA 1910–1930*. Exh. cat. Albuquerque: University of New Mexico Art Museum, 1967.

Novak, Barbara, *American Painting of the Nineteenth Century*, New York: Praeger Publishers, 1969, pp. 270–76.

Weaver, Mike, *William Carlos Williams: The American Background*, Cambridge, England: Cambridge University Press, 1971.

Avant-Garde Painting and Sculpture in America, 1910–1925. Exh. cat. Wilmington: Delaware Art Museum, 1975.

Rose, Barbara, *American Art Since 1900*, New York: Holt, Rinehart and Winston, 1975, pp. 80–91.

Tashjian, Dickran, *Skyscraper Primitives*, Middletown, Connecticut: Wesleyan University Press, 1975.

Taylor, Joshua C., *America as Art*, Washington, D.C.: Smithsonian Press, 1976, pp. 187–214.

Brown, Milton, "Precisionism and Mechanism," in *The Modern Spirit: American Painting, 1908–1935*. Exh. cat. London: Arts Council of Great Britain, 1977, pp. 52–55.

Homer, William Innes, *Alfred Stieglitz and the American Avant-Garde*, Boston: New York Graphic Society, 1977.

Maroney, Jay, *Lines of Power.* Exh. cat. New York: Hirschl & Adler Galleries, 1977.

Dijkstra, Bram, ed., *A Recognizable Image: William Carlos Williams on Art and Artists,* New York: New Directions, 1978.

Fillin-Yeh, Susan, *The Precisionist Painters 1916–1949: Interpretations of a Mechanical Age.* Exh. cat. Huntington: Heckscher Museum, 1978.

Tashjian, Dickran, *William Carlos Williams and the American Scene, 1920–1940,* New York: Whitney Museum of American Art, 1978.

Brown, Milton W., et al., *American Art,* New York: Harry N. Abrams, Inc., 1979.

Fillin-Yeh, Susan, "Charles Sheeler: Industry, Fashion, and the Vanguard," *Arts,* vol. 54, February 1980, pp. 154–58.

Doezema, Marianne, *American Realism and the Industrial Age.* Exh. cat. Cleveland: The Cleveland Museum of Art, 1980.

Schulz, Bernhard, "Made in America: Technik und Dingwelt im Präzisionismus," *Amerika: Traum und Depression 1920/40.* Exh. cat. Berlin: Neue Gesellschaft für bildende Kunst, 1980, pp. 72–137.

Zabel, Barbara, "The Precisionist-Constructivist Nexus: Louis Lozowick in Berlin," *Arts Magazine,* vol. 56, October 1981, pp. 123–27.

Brown, Milton W., "Le Réalisme aux États-Unis entre les deux guerres," in *Les Réalismes.* Exh. cat. Paris: Centre Georges Pompidou, 1981, pp. 240–42.

Davidson, Abraham, *Early American Modernist Painting 1910–1935,* New York: Harper & Row, 1981, pp. 182–228.

Pultz, John, and Catherine B. Scallen, *Cubism and American Photography, 1910–1930.* Exh. cat. Williamstown: Sterling and Francine Clark Institute, 1981.

Stewart, Patrick Leonard, "Charles Sheeler, William Carlos Williams, and the Development of the Precisionist Aesthetic, 1917–1931," Ph.D. diss., University of Delaware, Newark, 1981.

Kramer, Hilton, " 'Images of America': The Precisionists," *The New Criterion,* vol. 1, December 1982, pp. 48–53.

Zabel, Barbara, "The Machine as Metaphor, Model, and Microcosm: Technology and American Art, 1915–1930," *Arts Magazine,* vol. 57, December 1982, pp. 100–05.

Tsujimoto, Karen, *Images of America Precisionist Painting and Modern Photography.* Exh. cat. Seattle: University of Washington Press, 1982.

Platt, Susan, "Precisionism: America's Immaculates," *images & issues,* vol. 3, March/April 1983, pp. 22–23.

Stewart, Rick, "Charles Sheeler, William Carlos Williams, and Precisionism: A Redefinition," *Arts Magazine,* vol. 58, November 1983, pp. 100–114.

Menton, Seymour, *Magic Realism Rediscovered, 1918–1981,* Philadelphia: Art Alliance Press, 1983, pp. 71–81.

Platt, Susan Noyes, *Modernism in the 1920s: Interpretations of Modern Art from Expressionism to Constructivism,* Ann Arbor: UMI Research Press, 1985.

Banham, Reyner, *A Concrete Atlantis: U.S. Industrial Building and European Modern Architecture 1900–1925,* Cambridge, Massachusetts, and London: The MIT Press, 1986.

Green, Nancy E., *American Modernism: Precisionist Works on Paper.* Exh. cat. Ithaca: Herbert F. Johnson Museum of Art, Cornell University, 1986.

Kuenzli, Rudolf, ed., *New York Dada,* New York: Willis Locker and Owens, 1986.

Schleier, Merrill, *The Skyscraper in American Art, 1890–1931,* Ann Arbor: UMI Research Press, 1986.

Wilson, Richard Guy, et al., *The Machine Age in America 1918–1941.* Exh. cat. New York: Harry N. Abrams, Inc., in association with The Brooklyn Museum, 1986.

Baker, John, *Henry Lee McFee and Formalist Realism in American Still Life, 1923–1936,* Lewisburg: Bucknell University Press, and London and Toronto: Associated University Presses, 1987.

Steinman, Lisa M., *Made in America: Science, Technology, and American Modernist Poets,* New Haven: Yale University Press, 1987.

Tichi, Cecelia, *Shifting Gears: Technology, Literature, Culture in Modernist America,* Chapel Hill: The University of North Carolina Press, 1987.

Danly, Susan, and Leo Marx, eds., *The Railroad in American Art; Representations of Technological Change,* Cambridge, Massachusetts: The MIT Press, 1988.

Lubowsky, Susan, *Precisionist Perspectives: Prints and Drawings,* Exh. cat. New York: Whitney Museum of American Art at Phillip Morris, 1988.

Schmidt, Peter, *William Carlos Williams, the Arts, and Literary Tradition,* Baton Rouge: Louisiana State University Press, 1988.

Sayre, Henry M., "American Vernacular: Objectivism, Precisionism, and the Aesthetics of the Machine," *Twentieth-Century Literature,* vol. 35, Fall 1989, pp. 310–42.

Hambourg, Maria Morris, *The New Vision: Photography Between the World Wars,* New York: The Metropolitan Museum of Art, 1989.

Orvell, Miles, *The Real Thing: Imitation and Authenticity in American Culture, 1880–1940,* Chapel Hill: University of North Carolina Press, 1989.

Turner, Elizabeth Hutton, *American Artists in Paris 1919–1929,* Ann Arbor and London: UMI Research Press, 1989.

Rubin, Joan Shelley, "A Convergence of Vision: Constance Rourke, Charles Sheeler, and American Art," *American Art Quarterly,* vol. 42, June 1990, pp. 191–222.

Agee, William C., "Modern American Art: The First Half-Century," *Walker Art Center: Paintings and Sculpture from the Collection,* Minneapolis: Walker Art Center, 1990, pp. 52–53.

Berman, Avis, *Rebels on Eighth Street: Juliana Force and the Whitney Museum of American Art,* New York: Atheneum, 1990.

Fillin-Yeh, Susan, *The Technological Muse.* Exh. cat. Katonah: Katonah Museum of Art, 1990.

Clair, Jean, ed., *The 1920s: Age of the Metropolis.* Exh. cat. Montreal: The Montreal Museum of Fine Arts, 1991.

Lucic, Karen, *Charles Sheeler and the Cult of the Machine,* Cambridge, Massachusetts: Harvard University Press, 1991.

Harnsberger, R. Scott, *Ten Precisionist Artists. Annotated Bibliographies,* Westport, Connecticut: Greenwood Press, 1992.

Rosenblum, Robert, "Art: Precisionist Painting," *Architectural Digest*, March 1993, pp. 140–43.

Crunden, Robert M., *American Salons*, New York: Oxford University Press, 1993.

Mille, Diana Dimodica, "Precisionism in Perspective: Form and Philosophy in Twentieth-Century Art," Ph.D. diss., City University of New York, 1993.

Schmied, Wieland, "Precisionist View and American Scene: The 1920s," *American Art in the Twentieth Century*. Exh. cat. Munich: Prestel Verlag, 1993, pp. 47–59.

Smith, Terry, *Making the Modern: Industry, Art, and Design in America*, Chicago: The University of Chicago Press, 1993.

Sources at the Archives of American Art, Smithsonian Institution

Charles Daniel Papers, Roll 1343

Downtown Gallery Papers

Henry McBride Papers, Rolls NMcB2, NMcB3

Helen Appleton Read Papers, Roll N736

Charles Sheeler Papers

Forbes Watson Papers, Rolls D47, D48

Whitney Museum of American Art Papers

APPENDIX

Louis Lozowick, "The Americanization of Art," *Machine-Age Exposition*, New York: *Little Review*, 1927, pp. 18–19.

The history of America is a history of gigantic engineering feats and colossal mechanical construction. . . . The dominant trend in America today is towards an industrialization and standardization which require precise adjustment of structure to function which dictate an economic utilization of processes and materials and thereby foster in man a spirit of objectivity excluding all emotional aberration and accustom his vision to shapes and colors not paralleled in nature.

The dominant trend in America of today, beneath all the apparent chaos and confusion, is towards order and organization which find their outward sign and symbol in the rigid geometry of the American city: in the verticals of its smoke stacks, in the parallels of its car tracks, the squares of its streets, the cubes of its factories, the arc of its bridges, the cylinders of its gas tanks.

Upon this underlying mathematical pattern as a scaffolding may be built a solid plastic structure of great intricacy and subtlety. The artist who confronts his task with original vision and accomplished craftsmanship will note with exactitude the articulation, solidity, and weight of advancing and receding masses, will define with precision the space around objects and between them; he will organize line, plane, and volume into a well knit design. . . . The true artist will in sum objectify the dominant experience of our epoch in plastic terms that possess value for more than this epoch alone.

CHRONOLOGY

1915 In New York, Walter and Louise Arensberg launch their avant-garde salon, which includes Marcel Duchamp, Francis Picabia, Albert Gleizes, and Jean Crotti. Numerous articles proclaim New York as the world's new art center. Van Wyck Brooks's *America's Coming of Age* is published.

1916 Picabia has a major show of his mechanomorphic paintings in January at the Modern Gallery, New York. In March, Charles Sheeler is represented in New York in the Anderson Galleries' landmark *Forum Exhibition,* which stressed the American avant-garde. Morton Schamberg's pioneering Precisionist machine paintings are exhibited in a group show at the Bourgeois Galleries, New York, in April. He frequents the Arensberg salon, along with Charles Demuth, Sheeler, Joseph Stella, and William Carlos Williams.

1917 Photographs by Schamberg, Sheeler, and Paul Strand are featured in a three-man show in March–April at the Modern Gallery. Sheeler's works based on Bucks County barns and Demuth's architectural series created in Bermuda are significant, early examples of the Precisionist style. The term "precision" is applied to Sheeler's and Preston Dickinson's work. Duchamp's controversial readymade, *Fountain,* is rejected by the hanging committee of the first jury-free Society of Independent Artists exhibition in New York, which includes work by Davis, Demuth, O'Keeffe, Picabia, Schamberg, Sheeler, Stella, Stieglitz, and Strand.

1918 Amédée Ozenfant and Le Corbusier publish *Après le Cubisme* (After Cubism) in Paris as the manifesto of Purism. Alfred Stieglitz awards photography prizes to Sheeler, Schamberg, and Strand at the Wanamaker Salon in Philadelphia in March.

1920 Sheeler and Strand collaborate in making a film about New York City entitled *Manhatta.*

1921 *Manhatta* receives its first public screening in 1921 at the Rialto Theater on Broadway. Le Corbusier and Ozenfant publish their seminal essay, "Purism," in the January issue of *L'Esprit Nouveau.*

1922 Edward Weston travels from California to New York, where he meets Stieglitz, Georgia O'Keeffe, Sheeler, and Strand. Works by Edward Bruce, Stefan Hirsch, O'Keeffe, and Stella are exhibited in a group show of American painters at the Bourgeois Galleries in May and characterized by Forbes Watson as exemplary "of a contemporaneous new style in painting which may be called neo-primitive American."

1923 In March–April, the Bourgeois Galleries' annual exhibition features work by George Ault, Bruce, Hirsch, O'Keeffe, and Stella. They are regarded by the dealer Stephan Bourgeois as the heirs to the tradition of America's "primitive" painters. The Salons of America exhibition in May in New York juxtaposes machinery with work by Ault, Bruce, and Sheeler, whom Henry McBride refers to as the "Be Hard School." In May–June the Belmaison Gallery sponsors the first of three annual shows devoted to views of New York. Louis Lozowick's American City paintings are praised for their American vigor and precision when exhibited in the summer at the Galerie Alfred Heller, Berlin. In December, Demuth and Sheeler are recognized for their original contributions to the *Seven Americans* exhibition at the Galeries Durand-Ruel in Paris. Le Corbusier celebrates American industrial and urban architecture in *Vers une Architecture* (published in English in 1927 as *Towards a New Architecture*). Fernand Léger's "The Esthetics of the Machine" is published in the spring issue of *The Little Review.* Sheeler and Williams become close friends (the poet had already struck up a friendship with Demuth by 1903–4). Marianne Moore writes the poem "Bowls," employing the phrase: "I learn that we are precisians / not citizens of Pompeii arrested in action." She later changes the term to "precisionists."

1924 The Metropolitan Museum of Art, New York, founds its American Wing and Gertrude Vanderbilt Whitney's Studio Club presents the first significant exhibition of early American paintings, prints, carvings, and decorative art in February. Demuth and Sheeler are among the lenders to the show. German filmmaker Fritz Lang visits New York and conceives *Metropolis,* released three years later.

1925 The German *Neue Sachlichkeit* movement is inaugurated with the exhibition *"New Objectivity": German Painting Since Expressionism* at the Stadt Kunsthalle in Mannheim. The work of Lozowick is eventually included in the show, which is periodically reorganized during the summer months. Stieglitz organizes *Seven Americans* at the Anderson Galleries in March, which includes himself, Demuth, O'Keeffe, and Strand. Williams publishes his collection of essays *In the American Grain.*

1926 In January at a show at the Phillips Memorial Art Gallery, Washington, D.C., Duncan Phillips groups the architectural paintings of Dickinson, Demuth, Hirsch, Sheeler, and Spencer to demonstrate that "drastic modifications of the Cult of Cubism are being made in America." On January 23, the editors of *Art News,* Guy Eglington and Deoch Fulton, publish what may have been the first reference to "the Immaculate School" in a review of Sheeler's show at the New Art Circle in New York. Demuth, Dickinson, Lozowick, O'Keeffe, Spencer, and Stella are represented in the Société Anonyme's major *Exhibition of International Modern Art* at the Brooklyn Museum late in the year. The reestablishment of the German Bauhaus in Dessau marks a union of art and design with industry. An engineer and writer, John Riordan, sends Williams an essay on the latter's work entitled "The Theory and Practice of Precision Poetry," which features ideas based on the objectivist writings of Alfred North Whitehead.

1927 In January, Sheeler is declared the head of "the Sheeleresque Immaculate School" in an *Art News* review. In February, Dickinson and Spencer are classified as "our two foremost precisionists" by Louis Kalonyme in his review of the Whitney Studio Club's annual exhibition. Professor Alfred H. Barr Jr. refers to Sheeler and Dickinson as "Neo-Classicists" in the statement accompanying his *Progressive Modern Painting* exhibition at Wellesley College in April. In May, Barr lectures on "Tendencies in Modern American Painting" at Bowdoin College and discusses "the Precisionists . . . Charles Sheeler and Charles Demuth"—possibly the first official use of this term. Both painters serve, along with Duchamp, Lozowick, and Ralph Steiner, on the artists' organizing committee for the landmark *Machine-Age Exposition* in May at Steinway Hall in midtown Manhattan. Lozowick contributes to the accompanying catalogue an essay, "The Americanization of Art," that is later regarded as a manifesto for Precisionism as a machine aesthetic (see Appendix). During the fall, Sheeler spends six weeks in Detroit photographing the Ford Company's River Rouge plant—the world's largest, most technologically advanced industrial complex.

1928 The identity of the Daniel Gallery, New York, as the center for the Immaculates is established by reviews of a group exhibition held there in the fall. The term "immaculate school" is also extended to the work of artists outside of the Daniel Gallery, such as Ault and Hirsch.

1929 On May 1, Barr lectures on "Modern American Painting: A Cross-Section" at Wellesley College. He refers to Demuth, O'Keeffe, and Sheeler as "the Precisionists." Except for Sheeler, they are represented, along with Dickinson, at the newly founded Museum of Modern Art in its second exhibition, *Nineteen Living Americans*. Edward Weston serves as a consultant for the major *Film und Foto* exhibition in Stuttgart in June, which also includes photographs by Sheeler, Imogen Cunningham, Steiner, and Paul Outerbridge. Over four million automobiles are produced in America this year. Construction is begun on the Art Deco Chrysler Building in New York.

1930 In March, the Immaculates are viewed as "hold[ing] the fort" at the Daniel Gallery. In his book *Modern American Painters*, Samuel Kootz denigrates what he regards as the overly refined art of the "Immaculate School."

1931 Barr, now Director of The Museum of Modern Art, delivers a paper at the College Art Association conference, referring to Peter Blume, Dickinson, Charles Goeller, Hirsch, and Sheeler as New Objectivists participating in an international shift toward realism. The Objectivist movement is launched with a program and anthology of poems in the February issue of *Poetry* magazine, guest edited by Louis Zukofsky. Williams is briefly associated with this literary counterpart to Precisionism. The opening installation in November of the new Whitney Museum of American Art features Precisionist paintings by Demuth, Dickinson, Elsie Driggs, Sheeler, and Spencer. The newly erected Empire State Building becomes the tallest building in the world.

1932 With the closing of the Daniel Gallery in the Fall, Edith Halpert's Downtown Gallery becomes the primary showcase for artists working in Precisionist modes. Her colleague Holger Cahill writes an essay for The Museum of Modern Art's major survey of American art that fall with a section devoted to the Precisionists as "a group of painters who interpret the American scene with an austere realism." Also on view that fall are Precisionist paintings by Ault, Blume, Francis Criss, Demuth, Hirsch, Earl Horter, O'Keeffe, Sheeler, Spencer, and Arnold Wiltz in the Whitney Museum of American Art's first Biennial Exhibition.

1935 Sheeler is called the "precisionist par excellence" in January at the time of his joint exhibition with Charles Burchfield at the Detroit Society of Arts and Crafts. Halpert organizes a group show—including works by Davis, Sheeler, Spencer, and O'Keeffe—to challenge what she regards as the provincialism of the "Benton-Wood-Curry School." Her exhibition promoting the true, cosmopolitan American Scene coincides with the Whitney Museum's controversial survey of abstract painting in America, held in February–March, which includes work by Ault, Henry Billings, Davis, Demuth, Dickinson, Hirsch, Horter, O'Keeffe, Schamberg, Sheeler, Spencer, and Stella.

1936 James W. Lane identifies Demuth as a leading "Immaculate" in an important essay in *Masters of American Art* summarizing Demuth's accomplishments. Charlie Chaplin epitomizes the dehumanization of the assembly line in his film *Modern Times*.

1937 In a review of the Whitney Museum's annual exhibition, Margaret Breuning groups Niles Spencer and Francis Criss as Precisionists.

1938 The Museum of Modern Art organizes a survey of three centuries of American Art to send to the Musée du Jeu de Paume in Paris in May–July. In his introduction to the catalogue, Barr refers to "an 'immaculate' or 'precisionist' school of American painting," epitomized by "the extraordinary technical refinement of Demuth, Dickinson, Sheeler, and Blume."

1939 Peyton Boswell discusses the "precisionists" Blume, O'Keeffe, and Spencer in his book *Modern American Painting*. Lane praises Sheeler's "immaculatism" and "precision" in a review of the artist's retrospective at The Museum of Modern Art in the fall. Other critics such as Elizabeth McCausland accuse Sheeler of ignoring the tensions of the modern industrial world.

1941 The exhibition *A New Realism* features the work of Ralston Crawford, Demuth, Sheeler, and Spencer at the Cincinnati Art Museum in March–April.

1943 The Museum of Modern Art's survey *American Realists and Magic Realists* in February–March features work by Blume, Edmund Lewandowski, Lozowick, Sheeler, and Miklos Suba. In the exhibition catalogue, curator Dorothy Miller states that Sheeler, Demuth, Dickinson, and O'Keeffe were known as Precisionists before the end of the 1920s.

1945 Milton Brown, a graduate student at the Institute of Fine Arts, New York University, publishes the first substantive article on Precisionism, which he renames Cubist-Realism to denote the movement's general development "from the use of simple abstract surfaces to the meticulous rendering of nature."

1947 Wolfgang Born, an assistant professor of fine arts at Louisiana State University, publishes *Still Life Painting in America,* the first comprehensive study employing the term "Precisionism" to characterize this movement. In it, he discusses the work of Sheeler, Demuth, and Dickinson. He further develops his ideas on Precisionism in *American Landscape Painting,* published in 1948. In November, Halpert begins to promote as Precisionists certain Downtown Gallery artists including Sheeler, Crawford, Demuth, and Spencer, who has his first one-man show in many years.

1951 John I. H. Baur, curator of American art at the Brooklyn Museum, publishes *Revolution and Tradition in Modern Art,* in which he reverts to the usage of the "Immaculates" label.

1960 In November–December, Martin Friedman, acting director of the Walker Art Center, Minneapolis, presents the first comprehensive exhibition on Precisionism, *The Precisionist View in American Art,* with more than seventy works from 1915 to 1960 by sixteen painters.

1982 In September–November, the San Francisco Museum of Modern Art presents *Images of America: Precisionist Painting and Modern Photography,* curated by Karen Tsujimoto. It is the first exhibition to emphasize the integral connection between photography and Precisionist painting.

1983 Reviewing Tsujimoto's exhibition, Rick Stewart writes a seminal article (based upon his 1981 dissertation for the University of Delaware), "Charles Sheeler, William Carlos Williams, and Precisionism: A Redefinition." He proposes that Precisionism was "a definable style [based on] the adaptation of science-oriented methods to visual perception. . . . a fundamental reordering of reality brought about by the rise of an Objectivist aesthetic" in painting and literature.

INDEX

Numbers in *italics* indicate pages on which illustrations appear.

PHOTOGRAPH CREDITS

Armen, fig. 8; plates 11, 16, 53
Geoffrey Clements, fig. 12; plates 58, 70
Lee Clockman, plate 93
Sheldon Collins, New Jersey, plate 13
Joseph Crilley, plate 120
R. Echelmeyer, plate 43
Gamma One Conversions, New York, plate 32
Tom Loonan, plate 119
Andrew Lustbaum, plates 26–28, 30, 61, 63, 92, 99, 100, 105, 106
Robert E. Mates, copyright © The Solomon R. Guggenheim Foundation, New York, fig. 3
Josh Nefsky, New York, plates 18, 76
Joseph Painter Photography, Philadelphia, plate 33
Sandak/Macmillan, plates 50, 103
Steven Sloman, plate 23
Lee Stalsworth, plate 21
Soichi Sunami, New York, fig. 21
Sarah Wells, plate 79
Bruce M. White Photography, New York, plates 52, 130
Bill Witt, plate 118
Graydon Wood, fig. 1
Antje Zeis-Loi, copyright © Eva Grossberg, fig. 30
Zindman/Fremont, plate 80